SANGIN BEG
Sair-ul-Manazil

SANGIN BEG
Sair-ul-Manazil

Translated into English by
Nausheen Jaffery

Edited by
Swapna Liddle

with contributions from
Md. Ehteshamuddin
Akhlaque Ahmad ahan
Masood Alam Falahi
Amaal Akhtar
Shad Naved

Illustrations by
Neeti Banerji

Published by
Tulika Books
44 (first floor), Shahpur Jat
New Delhi 110 049, India
www.tulikabooks.in

© Tulika Books 2017

First edition (hardback) 2017

ISBN: 978-93-82381-86-0

Printed at Chaman Offset, Delhi 110 002

Contents

This is one of the most chosen ~~cities since~~ ancient days. In ~~historical records we often see~~
that from Hastinapur down to river Ganga there existed only one city ~~that is now called Delhi.~~
~~In the middle~~ of the plain ~~in which this city stands,~~ there flow the river Ganga and Yamuna.
After the ~~legendary~~ battle ~~of~~ Kaurav and Pandavas, this city was divided into two parts, i.e.
Hastinapur, which is still known ~~with its former name;~~ ~~while the other part got fame with its~~
~~new name i.e.~~ Indraprastha. After a long period, a big landlord, whose name was ~~inhabited a~~
village in Indrapatha ~~and called it, Delhi, which later expanded and became very popular. Since~~
~~then the population of this place started to increase day by day~~ ~~and expanded so much so that in~~
the year 429 ~~according to Bikramji Calendar,~~ the king Angpal of Tur tribe, ~~established one city~~
~~with the same name for their dynasties and rulership.~~
~~When Sultan Mahmud of Ghazna ransacked Delhi, it~~ was ruled by ~~king~~ Mahipal and his son
~~Indrapal.~~ Mahmud attacked many cities ~~located between~~ Kanauj and Somnath, but he never ~~paid~~
his ~~attention~~ towards Delhi.

Sultan of ~~Shuhda~~ the king of ~~the martyrs,~~ Salaar Masood Ghazi came to ~~this region~~ and
~~made attacks on~~ its ruler, Raja Mahipal, who was badly injured, ~~and thus~~ vacated the city. ~~But he~~
died on ~~his~~ way. His son, ~~Indrapal~~ damaged the face of Salaar Masud and made ~~an~~ escape. ~~It from~~
~~was after that Muslims got peace in this city.~~
~~Though the~~ People of Delhi requested ~~to~~ Salaar Masud to issue coins and ~~read Khutba~~ in his name but
being a ~~close~~ relative of Sultan Mahmud, ~~from his maternal side~~ he didn't accept this proposal.
He ~~appointed some~~ muslim ~~officials~~ in Delhi and went ~~with others towards Europe.~~
~~Sultan of Shuhda~~ Masud Ghazi, commonly called "Rajab Salaar", "Ghazi Miyan" and "Bala
Miyan" was assassinated in Behraich near Surajkund ~~and thus~~ Delhi again ~~came~~ under the rule
of ~~Tur tribe. Rai Pathura~~ who ~~was~~ known as Prithviraj belongs to ~~the~~ same tribe.
In the year 1200 ~~(according to Vikramajit Calendar),~~ Rai Pathura built ~~one~~ palace near the
~~place now called~~ Mahrauli ~~in his name~~ and appointed ~~here~~ his brother Khande Rao as his
deputy. In 588 A.H. (1192 A.D.) when Sultan Shahabuddin Ghauri ~~got victory~~ over Raipathura,
the rulership of Hindus came to an end, ~~after their rule~~ for 16 years, 4 months and 3 days.

Sultan Shahabuddin Ghauri appointed one of his ~~renounced~~ slaves, ~~namely~~ Qutbuddin Aibek,
~~as the Governor of the Sultanate of~~ Hindustan and returned to Ghazna. Qutbuddin was called
Aibek, because one ~~of the~~ finger ~~of both~~ ~~the~~ hands was ~~cut~~ and ~~became famous with this nick~~
~~name.~~ Sultan Qutbuddin Aibek captured the fort of Delhi in a very short time and ~~made~~ Delhi
~~the seat of Muslim rule~~ in 591 A.H. (1195 A.D)

Sultan Qutbuddin Aibek and Sultan Iutmish ~~both built~~ Quwatul-Islam mosque and ~~a~~ minarate
near the shrine of Khwaja Qutbuddin by ~~removing idols on the site of~~ Rajpathura ~~fort.~~ These

The Journey of a Text

NARAYANI GUPTA

Before tourist guidebooks appeared, there were descriptions of Indian towns by visitors from other parts of the subcontinent, and from overseas. One such is this book, written two hundred years ago.

It is wonderful to follow the life of a text – *Sair-ul-Manazil* was written in Persian in 1821. It was a slim book, the kind that gets mislaid in a pile of heavier books. I do not know how many copies are extant. Dr Sharif Husain Qasimi, by translating it into Urdu in 1981, made it accessible to many readers. After this, it was only natural to hope it could be made available in an English version. Of course, there were accounts of late-Mughal Delhi written by English visitors and administrators, but they saw the city so differently from the way Indians did.

In 1997 Nausheen Jaffery, niece of Dr Yunus Jaffery, the legendary teacher of Persian at Zakir Husain/Delhi College, was in the first year of her MA in the Department of History and Culture at Jamia Millia Islamia, where I was on the faculty. Nausheen often dropped in for a chat, and talked animatedly about her plans to travel, to study abroad, to write. After her exams, she asked me to suggest something she could do as a vacation project. I suggested she read the Urdu version of *Sair*, and perhaps translate it into English. She liked the idea, and two months later proudly brought me a handwritten translation. I was delighted, but advised her to put it aside till she was through with her MA. Immediately after that, she began to work on her M Phil dissertation, which was on a subject very dear to her, the Mughal princess Jahan Ara Begum. She completed a remarkably good thesis, and was dreaming about doctoral work and of going abroad, when the blow struck. She was diagnosed with cancer. Between then and 27 November 2004, when she was relieved from her terrible suffering, was a period from which I would only like to remember her unwavering courage, good humour and concern for others. Equally heartwarming was the way her friends and teachers, and the scholars whom her uncle had initiated into Persian, rallied and contributed generously.

My colleague Professor Azizuddin, who had been her supervisor, decided to publish her work on Jahan Ara. One day, months after she had gone, I looked at the pencilled pages of her translation. Her labours of translation too should not be forgotten. I turned to Swapna Liddle who, like Nausheen, was a research scholar in our Department, working on a history of nineteenth-century Delhi. She very generously agreed to go through Nausheen's draft and fill in the gaps. The narrative was interleaved with the text of verses and inscriptions in Persian, and prayers in Arabic, which were translated with the help of scholars whom Swapna lists in the Introduction. Just as so many people rallied so naturally to Nausheen's side when she lay ill in hospital, so too people came forward naturally to help her book forward.

I can see her raising her eyebrows and smiling in amusement, as I try to account for the unconscionable delay in the book appearing in print. Again, what I remember is not the delays, but the delightful way in which the text morphed from pencil writing to computer printouts, how the highlighted gaps for Arabic texts slowly disappeared and were replaced by translations, how Swapna's daughter contributed the sketches that lightened the printed pages, and, most miraculous of all, the calm and gently humorous way Indu and her team saw to it that the flame did not go out.

Here, then, is the work of many hands, to craft a lamp that will light up the *chowks* and the *galis* of the wondrous city of Shahjahanabad of which we catch only glimpses today. All because twenty years ago a young girl who lived in Shahjahanabad, eager to do something useful during a long summer vacation, stood smiling at the door of my study, saying, 'Ma'am, may I come in?'

That young girl comes to life overleaf, in a poignant essay by Alice Albinia.

Recollections of Nausheen

ALICE ALBINIA

नौशीन अपने
भाई के साथ

Nausheen with her brother

I first met Nausheen Jaffery when I was nineteen years old and she was twenty-two. I was visiting India before beginning at Cambridge University, and she, already a student in Delhi, was deputed by her uncle, Dr Yunus Jaffery, to take me on a tour of the city. So we went to the places she loved most and considered vital to my education: the Red Fort, Humayan's tomb, the Jama Masjid. It was the first time I had ever been to a mosque and I remember it vividly: the cool of the place (it was summertime), the seriousness of the worshippers, how clean and uncluttered it was. We climbed one of the minarets and looked down at Old Delhi – at the mesh of streets where Nausheen had been raised and still lived with her family. This was her city, and she spoke of it with fond irritation, as one might of a cranky old relative (Nausheen had many relatives). Prayer-time came, and we descended to the main hall; she thought it important for me to witness how Muslims organized themselves in worship. But one of the mosque caretakers hurried over, scolding her for bringing a foreigner, a non-believer, into this place at this time. Nausheen, who was never cowed by what other people thought, told the man in her best haughty manner that actually I was Turkish (not true), that I was visiting Delhi to renew my faith (not true either), and that he should leave us alone. Chastised, the man turned away, and we lingered at the back of the hall as worshippers began streaming in through the mosque's two open gates. We left before the prayers began, but she was pleased that I had been present in an inclusive way at this holy place. It was a formative moment. Nausheen: a gentle, mischievous guide to what was then, to me, her mysterious faith and culture.

Four years later, after graduating from university, I moved to Delhi to work as an editor and journalist. I began thinking about the two books I would go on to write about the region. By then Nausheen was studying for her MA degree, and we would meet for lunch at a south Indian place she liked near Connaught Place. She was full of confidence. Always opinionated, always independent, always perfectly elegant and strong-minded as she negotiated the city – observing the etiquette of both its *muhallas*, and the research libraries and universities where she planned to carve out her singular career. She was clear about the shape her life would take. There was something unusual, wonderful, about her determination. For Nausheen there would be no conventional path into marriage and motherhood. She was learning Persian under the tutelage of her uncle, and above all she wanted to continue his work, translating from and writing about Indo–Persian texts and culture.

When she began researching the history of Jahan Ara Begum, the intellectual daughter of the Mughal emperor Shah Jahan, we visited the princess's grave which was walking distance from my flat. This place, the shrine of the Sufi saint Nizam-ud-Din, became a reference point for me when I wrote my first novel. When I was asked to write a piece on Islamic education, Nausheen accompanied me to a series of *madrasas* across the city. We visited institutions of varying quality and lineage: some venerable and elegant with quiet red sandstone courtyards and important libraries, others crammed into insalubrious corners of down-at-heel housing colonies. At each place Nausheen was polite and firm, and it was instructive to see how she dealt with the series of pious and evasive Islamic teachers. Nothing seemed to faze her; especially not the startled looks of the religious men she cross-questioned. This experience too I recalled later, on trips to *madrasas* over the border, in Karachi and the Swat valley, when I was researching my book on the Indus valley.

Because Nausheen used to complain about the difficulty of concentrating on her work at home in the old city – it was the pigeon-flyers, she said, who made the most racket – I offered her the spare room in my quiet *barsati*. She came for a week but soon got homesick (for her family, for her mother's cooking, for the air conditioner in her bedroom). She was devoted to her family – her scholar–uncle, her two brothers who were running the electrician's store below the house, her sister Simin who was busy doing social work in women's reproductive health, her beloved mother (whose complicated, delicious recipe for biryani Nausheen had sent me while I was still in Cambridge, subsisting on a non-gourmet student diet), and later, her sister-in-law Shazia, whose spirit was as self-sufficient as her own.

After I returned to London to study at SOAS, I visited Delhi during the Christmas holidays, and Nausheen found me a room to rent in her aunt's house, a few streets away from hers. During those three weeks, I understood why the old city had lured her back. Every evening, after a day of research in the library, I would step from the wide polluted roads of murky New Delhi into a dazzle of brightly-lit, winding streets. There were no cars: instead a harmonious cacophony of scooter horns, temple bells, hawkers' cries. There was a city-village smell of spices and cow-dung. The shops sold wonderful things such as copper colanders or embroidered leather slippers. Because it was wedding season and my wardrobe was inadequate for the parties we were bound to attend, Nausheen gave me a heavy pink brocade-silk *salwar kameez*. Now, each time I take it out of my silver Delhi trunk, it reminds me of that winter. Of family dinners at her house; of Nausheen laughing with her siblings; of life under the looming beauty of the Friday mosque. This was the world I was shown.

Always, while performing her duties as a loving daughter, niece, sister, friend, Nausheen lived for her work. She always spoke with enthusiasm and pride of the research she was doing; and right up to the end, even when she was too ill to move from her bed, she was making plans for the next project, the next translation. Like her uncle Dr Jaffery, Nausheen wanted to bring the literary culture of Delhi's past alive. It is a wonderful testament to her determined spirit – as well as to the affection and respect she evinced in her colleagues – that both her historical work on Jahan Ara Begum and her translation of *Sair-ul-Manazil* have been published after her death. I am sure that Nausheen herself would be delighted at how magnificently her work lives on to encourage others in their explorations. Indeed, I am sure she would have expected nothing less. It would have been lovely to witness her pride.

Editor's Introduction

SWAPNA LIDDLE

Written in the 1820s, *Sair-ul-Manazil* ('a tour of the mansions') was, as far as we know, the first attempt to systematically list the monuments of Delhi. Apart from public buildings like mosques, temples, shrines and tombs, it listed wells, gardens, houses, shops and stray graves. This was in itself a formidable task, and one that might easily have resulted in a very dry and tedious document. The author, however, considerably enlivened it by a description of the various localities of the city, of the people who lived and worked there in his time, social activities and fairs, and historical anecdotes connected with places and people.

We do not know much about the man who wrote the book. Even his name, in different manuscripts of the book, is variously written as Sangin Beg and Sangi Beg. Sangi Beg is a somewhat more likely name, and a historical person by that name was around in Delhi in the 1830s. Frustratingly, however, we know hardly anything about that person either so it is impossible to say if they were the same. For the time being, therefore, it is convenient to use the name Sangin Beg simply because it has more frequently been cited as the name of the author of this book.

In the nineteenth century the heart of the city was Shahjahanabad, and though the English East India Company was virtual ruler of both city and empire, reality was softened by the continuing use of the name of the Mughal emperor in all official business. As such, the city was still frequently referred to as the *Dar-ul-Khilafa*, or capital. Using this walled city as a starting point, Sangin Beg creates a verbal map and we are taken up high streets, into lanes and down highways, as he points out to us buildings and other features of interest on the way.

We hear of many people. Some of these were important personages – rich merchants, important officials, *nawabs*, famous poets and *hakims*. There are also many who would never find their way into any conventional history book, but were nevertheless important to the life of the city, and their houses and shops are pointed out to us as landmarks. Thus we learn of the *rewdiwala* who had his shop north of Hauz Qazi, the goldsmith who had his house close to Turkman Gate, Roshan *mochi* who lived in Pahadi Bhojla, Fateh Ji and Karim Ji turban sellers located to the south of the Jama Masjid, the shop of Kanjas, a famous *halwai* in Dariba, the house of Puran the tailor also near Dariba, the courtesans Lachhmi and Bi Jan, and Hafiz Ilahi Bakhsh the pedlar next to Fatehpuri Masjid.

We get a glimpse of the lively social and cultural scene at the many public spaces within the city. The most prominent among these was the area surrounding the Jama Masjid. On the very steps of the mosque every evening pedlars would set up their stalls selling all manner of street food, cloth, exotic birds and animals, books and weapons. This was also where entertainers such as *madaris* (entertainers usually with animals) and *dastangos* (storytellers) would ply their trade.

Sangin Beg's main aim of course was the listing of buildings and this is by far the most substantial part of the work. He painstakingly recorded the location and history of hundreds of buildings, and above all copied their inscriptions. This was a valuable treasure for a posterity that would witness the destruction of many of these edifices.

The impetus behind Sangin Beg's account was in fact a need of the colonial state. The government of the East India Company was slowly but surely establishing its control over various categories of public property. The authorities were particularly interested in details of ownership, trusts and endowments. One of the first steps to be taken was a comprehensive documentation. While Charles Metcalfe was still the Resident (he left Delhi in December 1818) Sangin Beg had been commissioned to produce a document, in his own words, on the 'history and state of the deserted mosques, tombs and buildings of Shahjahanabad'. In fact, Sangin Beg's brief was very limited though he went considerably beyond it in *Sair-ul-Manazil*. Details of people and their occupations, descriptions of historic events, were incidental to the purposes of Metcalfe and his assistant, William Fraser, both of whom are mentioned as being responsible for engaging the author for this work.

The language of *Sair-ul-Manazil* is Persian, the language of culture and official business at the time. A publication of the text in 1982 contains an excellent introduction and translation into Urdu by Dr Sharif Husain Qasimi.[1]

It is a difficult text to translate. There are hundreds of proper names and titles, and many literary and religious allusions that have to be rendered intelligible to a readership that is not familiar with the background. Nausheen was a competent scholar and had done a good job of the text. Unfortunately, she was unable to complete an important part of the work – the translation of the inscriptions. My own competence is wholly inadequate to deal with the task, so in the first instance I filled in some of the gaps with the help of translations in a published listing of Delhi's monuments carried out by Zafar Hasan in the second decade of the twentieth century.[2] However, important translations still remained to be done, and this lack was made up by the efforts of Dr Md. Ehteshamuddin, Assistant Professor, Institute of Persian Research, Aligarh Muslim University and Dr Akhlaque Ahmad ahan, Associate Professor, Centre of Persian and Central Asian Studies, Jawaharlal Nehru University, who translated them into Urdu. These were then translated into English by Amaal Akhtar and Shad Naved. Invaluable help with translation from the Arabic was provided by Professor Masood Alam Falahi.

Chronograms are an important part of a large majority of the inscriptions. A chronogram is a form of mnemonic, at the foundation of which is the understanding that every letter is accorded a fixed numerical value. A short sentence or phrase, descriptive of the context, is composed in such a manner that a date, or more exactly

---

[1] Dr Sharif Husain Qasimi, ed., Mirza Sangin Beg, *Sair-ul-Manazil* (Persian text with Urdu translation), New Delhi, 1982.

[2] Zafar Hasan, *Monuments of Delhi*, Aryan Books, New Delhi, 2008 (reprint of 1916 edition).

a year, can be deciphered from it. The chronogram may form part of an inscription on a grave, tomb, mosque or other building, or it may simply live on in people's memory as the remembrance of an important day. The best chronograms are delightfully pithy. An excellent example is the chronogram for the year of the death of Humayun – 'The emperor Humayun fell from the roof', which gives the year 962, i.e. 1556–57.

In the translations, inscriptions have been set apart. I have made minimal modifications to Zafar Hasan's translation, very occasionally where I think that a meaning might be made clearer without the danger of it being distorted.

Most of the buildings Sangin Beg mentions are associated with particular people – builders of places of worship, occupants of houses and shops, etc. While he gave accounts for historical figures, he did not feel it necessary to give any biographical information for contemporaries or near-contemporaries. The readership Sangin Beg was addressing lived in a city with a population of around a hundred thousand, and it could be safely assumed that no introductions were needed. This is certainly not the case for us, separated as we are from the world of Sangin Beg by almost two centuries. I have tried, wherever possible, to add biographical details as footnotes. For these I have relied on a few basic works – Zafar Hasan's listing, Syed Ahmad Khan's *Asar-us-Sanadid*, Beale's *Oriental Biographical Dictionary*, Shahnawaz Khan's *Ma'asir-al-Umara*, Sadia Dehlvi's *The Sufi Courtyard*, Zill-ur-Rahman's *Dilli aur Tibb-e-Unani*, and Shama Mitra Chenoy's *Shahjahanabad: A City of Delhi*.[3]

Lastly, I have added a few comments about the present state of some of the sites that have changed considerably since Sangin Beg's time.

---

[3] Syed Ahmad Khan, *Asar-us-Sanadid*, Urdu Academy, Delhi, 2000; Thomas William Beale, *The Oriental Biographical Dictionary*, The Asiatic Society of Bengal, Calcutta, 1881; Baini Prashad and H. Beveridge, trans., Shahnawaz Khan's *Maathir-ul-Umara*, Janaki Prakashan, Patna, 1979; Sadia Dehlvi, *The Sufi Courtyard: Dargahs of Delhi*, Harper Collins, New Delhi, 2012; Hakeem S. Zill-ur-Rahman, *Dilli aur Tibb-e-Unani*, Urdu Academy, Delhi 1995; Shama Mitra Chenoy, *Shahjahanabad: A City of Delhi, 1638–1857*, Munshiram Manoharlal, New Delhi, 1998.

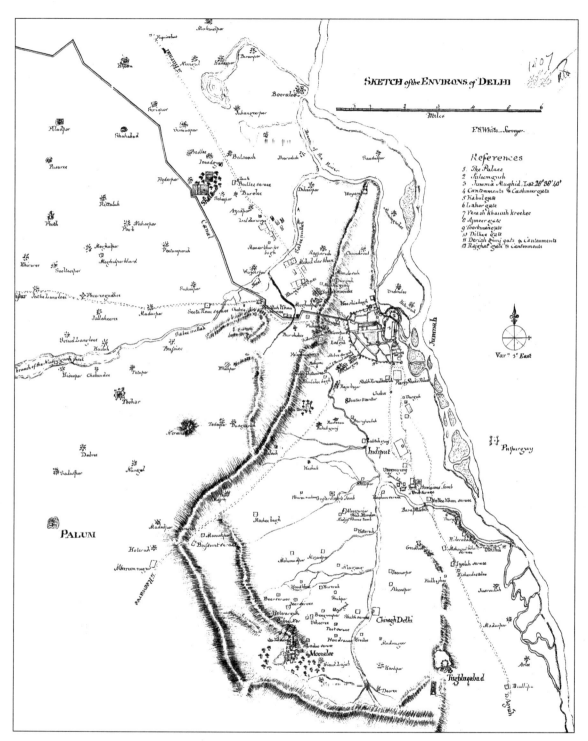

A map of Delhi in 1807

SANGIN BEG
Sair-ul-Manazil

I begin in the name of Allah, Most Gracious, Most Merciful.[1] He is that builder who by saying 'Be!' formed the universe with thousands of embellishments. He established the lofty house of creation on the walls of the elements and the pillars of the three kingdoms of nature (animal, vegetable, mineral). He adorned the high dome of the sky with stars. He illuminated the artistically crafted dome of the sky with the skylight of the sun. Any description of this builder is like a high fortress, the battlements of which the swift flying pigeon of vision and conception cannot reach. His definition and description is like a tall palace, so that the bird of imagination and ideas cannot reach its pinnacle. On the mosque of God's oneness is inscribed, 'Say: He is Allah, the One and Only.'[2] The Ka'ba of his description is decorated with the epithet, 'Allah, the Eternal, Absolute' [112:2].

He is that spring that has made death the means of release from the prison of pollution. He has entrusted the order of the world to the race of men. He has laid the foundation of this joyous population in the transitory house of this world. Do you not know that if the being of the flower were not dispersed, the branch of life would not bear fruit? A living creature is such a fruit that if it did not go into the next world, it would be called unripe. He is that disciple possessed of breath that if he did not

---

[1] In keeping with the practice of literary writing at the time, Sangin Beg begins with praises of God (Allah) and the Prophet, quoting several verses from the Quran.

[2] All English renderings of the verses of the Quran are taken from Abdullah Yusuf Ali, *The Meanings of the Holy Quran* (112:1); available at: http://www.islam101.com/quran/yusufAli/index.htm. All subsequent references to the Quran are given in square brackets in the main text.

annihilate himself in his saintly guide, which is this world, he would be found wanting. 'It is He who giveth life and who taketh it, and to Him shall ye all be brought back.' [10:56] The history of a man's birth and death according to his understanding and comprehension is this: 'From a sperm-drop He hath created him, and then moulded him in due proportions; Then doth He make His path smooth for him; Then He causeth him to die, and putteth him in his grave.' [80:19–21] He gave the keys to the fortress of existence to man. It may happen that one day He may destroy the sanctuary of this existence with the flood of 'Wherever ye are, death will find you out, even if ye are in towers built up strong and high!' [4:78] He may reprimand a people, saying, 'The mutual rivalry for piling up (the good things of this world) diverts you from the more serious things, until ye visit the graves.' [102:1–2] He will bring down punishment on them, as it is said, 'On them is the curse; for them is the terrible home!' [13:25] He may honour one group with regard and dignity, saying, 'Those are the ones who will be rewarded with the highest place in heaven.' [25:75] He may spare them, for 'The righteous will be amid gardens and fountains of clear-flowing water. Their greeting will be: "Enter ye here in peace and security."' [15:45–46]

[Verses]

[1] Allah is matchless. He is known as our lord and saviour and friend.

[2] He is the Lord of the Time, because of whom the world got its name. It is because of him that the sky and the land are at rest.

[3] He [who] is brave and perseveres, God grants him further heights and he [who] is arrogant, God destroys his arrogance.

The embellishments of praise and description are the adornment of His divine throne. The twelve immovable bastions of this sky constantly affirm its nine-chambered arch. The nine bases of the sky have the position of the pedestal of His high throne. Countless benedictions on the family of the beneficent and those of the highest position! On the pillars of their endeavours the strong fortress of the true faith is firmly established. The strong forts of the faith are firm because of their devoted efforts.

After the praise of God and encomiums of His Prophet, Sangin Beg, son of 'Ali Akbar Beg, says that these inscriptions are related to the history and a report of the condition of the deserted mosques, tombs and buildings of Shahjahanabad. This despairing recluse made a great effort and did a deep study of the buildings of Dehli [Delhi]. I copied each inscription exactly. With regard to most of these I made enquiries from Nawab Shams-ud-Daulah Zulfiqar-ul-Mulk Mirza Mahmud Khan Bahadur Zafar Jang Moosvi al-Husaini. The said Nawab Sahib is from Iran and unique in this *Dar-ul-Khilafa* [seat of the caliphate]. He has deeply studied books of history. His memory is wonderful. He holds the position of *bakhshi* in the service of Abul-Muzaffar Mu'in-ud-Din Muhammad Akbar Shah Badshah Ghazi.[3] After that I have committed these inscriptions and accounts to paper, and have called the book *Sair-ul-Manazil*. The reason for this labour and toil was the felicitous command of the noble, the refuge of the poor, Mr Charles Theophilus Metcalfe[4] Sahib and Mr William Fraser Sahib[5] – may their honour be on the ascendant, may their prosperity be sublime, may the shadow of their benevolence persist – the performance of which was binding. The justice of these grand Sahibs has caused the ruined hearts of the oppressed to prosper. Their impartiality has brought salvation to the world from the thorns of tyranny. The rain-clouds of their generosity have irrigated the fields of the people's stores. The pearls of their boundless favour have made the shells of sense and understanding free of want. The sun of their beneficence and favour has not left a single particle unilluminated. The showers of their bounty have made each person prosperous. They are the epitome of gentleness and tolerance, and are included in the high nobles. They are as wise and learned as Aristotle, as powerful and imbued with authority as Alexander. They are the patrons of the courts of law and the cherishers of justice. With their being they have given grace and elegance to the seat of government and fortune. The hall of rank and dignity is adorned by their personalities. Their being is no less than a bolt of lightning

---

[3] The Mughal emperor better known as Akbar II, son of Shah 'Alam II, reigned from 1806 to 1837. The emperor's *bakhshi* was the paymaster of the troops.

[4] Charles Metclafe was one of the best known early British administrators in Delhi. He eventually rose to the position of acting Governor General of India and, at the end of his career, Governor General of Canada. For general biographical details, see Edward Thompson, *The Life of Charles, Lord Metcalfe*, London, 1927. Specifically for details of his administration in Delhi, see Percival Spear, *Twilight of the Mughuls*, Oxford University Press, New Delhi, 1973.

[5] Fraser spent much of his civil service career in Delhi, rising to the highest post, that of Commissioner and Agent to the Governor General, in Delhi. He was assassinated in 1835, and Shams-ud-Din Khan, the Nawab of Firozpur Jhirka, was found guilty of conspiracy to have him killed, and was hanged.

for the harvests of the oppressors. For mischief-makers they are a destroying flood. The justice of Nausherwan has vowed that it will not swear by anything but their authority. The generosity of Hatim has sworn that it will sing praises of their essence and liberality alone. Sahban acknowledges their eloquence and Hassan their rhetoric.[6] These excellent gentlemen had expressed a desire that a report on Dehli [Delhi] and its buildings should be put together and submitted to them. As I am in their debt for many favours, I compiled and humbly submitted this book, which is like a picture that has no value before the Chinese emperor, and a gnat, which is nothing before Solomon.[7]

A Brief History of Dehli

This is a chosen city among the ancient cities. In several history books it is written that this side of the river Ganga, from Hastinapur down to Dehli, there existed only one territory, and the rivers Ganga and Jamuna flowed through the midst of it. After the battle between the Kauravs and the Pandavs this territory was divided into two parts. Hastinapur continued to be known by its old name, and Dehli became famous as Inderpat. After a long period a big landlord, whose name was Dihlu, settled a village in Inderpat, and this village came to be known as Dehli. From then on Dehli's population expanded day by day till in the year 429 Sammat Bikramjiti [Vikram Samvat], the Tur king Anangpal raised the standard of his rule and established a very big city near Inderpat, which came to be known by this name.[8] Several kings made it their capital.

During the rule and conquests of Sultan Mahmud Ghazi Ghaznavi, Dehli was ruled by Mahipal and his son Anangpal. Mahmud attacked several times many cities of Hindustan from Kannauj to Somnath, but did not turn towards Dehli. The Sultan-ush-

---

[6] In his hyperbolic praises of his patrons, Sangin Beg compares them to heroes of Persian and Arabian history, familiar characters to all who were well-versed in Persian literature. Nausherwan 'the just' was a sixth-century Sassanian ruler; Hatim Tai a historical figure of sixth-century Arabia, known for his generosity; Sahban Wa'il an ancient Arab figure proverbial for his eloquence; and Hassan ibn Thabit a companion of the Prophet Muhammad who also wrote poetry in the latter's defence.

[7] The Chinese emperor who was proud of his people's skill in making paintings and the gnat's tale which comes before Solomon complaining of the wind are both from the *Masnavi* of Maulana Rumi.

[8] Here Sangin Beg follows the accounts given in several of the popular Persian-language histories current in his time, including that of Abul Fazal and Muhammad Qasim Farishta. It is a mix of popular tradition, myth and history. For a history of early Delhi and the establishment of the city by Anangpal Tomar, see Upinder Singh, *Ancient Delhi*, Oxford University Press, New Delhi, 1999, especially pp. 28–38, 88–94.

Shuhada [King of Martyrs] Salar Mas'ud Ghazi[9] came to Dehli and engaged in battle with its ruler Raja Mahipal, who was badly injured. He left the city but died on his way. His son Anangpal wounded the face, nose and lips of Salar Mas'ud and made his escape. From that auspicious day Muslims began to dwell in Dehli.

The people of Dehli requested Salar Mas'ud to issue coins and have the *khutba* read in his name, but since his mother was a relative of Sultan Mahmud, out of regard for him, he did not accept this proposal. He left behind some leading Muslims in Dehli and went westwards.

The Sultan-ush-Shuhada Mas'ud Ghazi, commonly called Rajab Salar, Ghazi Miyan and Bala Miyan by the Hindustanis, was assassinated in Bahraich near Surajkund. In this way Dehli again came under the rule of the Turs. But soon after, this tribe lost control of Dehli to the Chauhan tribe. Rai Pithora, who is famous as Prithviraj, belonged to this tribe.

In the year 1200 Sammat, Rai Pithora[10] built a fort and a city after his own name near *mauza*-e-Mehrauli [village of Mehrauli], and there appointed his brother Khande Rao. In 588 [1192–93], when Sultan Shihab-ud-Din Ghori[11] was victorious over Rai Pithora, the rule of the Hindus came to an end. Rai Pithora ruled for sixteen years, four months and three days.

Sultan Shihab-ud-Din Ghori appointed one of his emancipated slaves, Qutb-ud-Din Aibak, his viceroy in Hindustan and returned to Ghazni. Qutb-ud-Din Aibak was his actual name. He was called 'Aibak' because one finger each of both his hands was missing. I read this in a book and therefore mention it here. Malik Qutb-ud-Din Aibak conquered the fort of Dehli and its surroundings in a very short time, and in this way Dehli became the seat of Muslim rulers in 591 [1195–96].

---

[9] Salar Mas'ud Ghazi's historicity is doubtful as he is not mentioned in any of the contemporary chronicles dealing with Mahmud Ghaznavi, whose nephew he is believed to be. Nevertheless a strong cult projecting him as a warrior developed from the seventeenth century onwards, centred in Bahraich in present-day Uttar Pradesh. For the cult of Ghazi Miyan, see the recent work by Shahid Amin, *Conquest and Community: The Afterlife of Warrior Saint Ghazi Miyan*, Orient Blackswan, New Delhi, 2015.

[10] This refers to the Chauhan ruler Prithviraj III (1177–1192). More accurately, the Chauhans extended the fort built by the Tomars. For Chauhan rule in Delhi, see Singh, *Ancient Delhi*, pp. 97–98; Satish Chandra, *Medieval India: From Sultanat to the Mughals, Part I: Delhi Sultanat (1206–1526)*, Har-Anand Publications, New Delhi, 1997, p. 23.

[11] He was also known as Muhammad Ghori.

Sultan Qutb-ud-Din Aibak and Sultan Shams-ud-Din Altamash[12] had the Quwwat-ul-Islam mosque and the *minar*[13] built near the shrine of Hazrat Khwaja Qutb-ud-Din[14] by demolishing temples and the palace of Rai Pithora. These will be mentioned in later pages. Both these Sultans used to live in the fort of Rai Pithora. Sultan Aibak had a palace called Qasr-e-Safed [the white palace] built in this fort.

Sultan Nasir-ud-Din Mahmud[15] had a building called Hazar Sutun [thousand pillars] built, which was completed during the reign of Sultan Ghiyas-ud-Din Balban.

Sultan Ghiyas-ud-Din Balban, during his rule, laid the foundation of a new fort in 666 [1267–68], which became famous by the name of Marzghan. This ruler also established a city that was called Ghiyaspur. This city was located where the *dargah* of Hazrat Nizam-ud-Din Auliya is situated.[16]

Sultan Kaiqubad, during his reign, in 668 [1269–70], built a city on the bank of the Jamuna with many attractive buildings and named it Kilokhari.[17] It was situated where today the perfumed dome and illuminated grave of Naseer-ud-Din Muhammad Humayun, Badshah-e-Ghazi [the conquering emperor], Jannat Ashiyani,[18] is located. This tomb will be mentioned at its appropriate place.

Sultan Jalal-ud-Din Khilji,[19] entitled Shaista Khan, during his reign, laid the foundation of another city called Koshak-e-Lal. After him, 'Ala-ud-

---

12 Commonly known to students of Indian history as Iltutmish (r. 1211–36).

13 This is the Qutub Minar and its adjoining mosque.

14 Qutb-ud-Din Bakhtiyar 'Kaki' who established the Chishti Sufi order in Delhi. He died in 1236, and his shrine attracts devotees to this day.

15 The grandson of Iltutmish, who reigned from 1246 to 1266, but the real power behind the throne was his father-in-law, Ghiyas-ud-Din Balban, who, after the death of Nasir-ud-Din, formally assumed the title of Sultan and reigned till his death in 1287.

16 Nizam-ud-Din Auliya is the revered Chishti Sufi saint who died in 1325.

17 Kaiqubad was the grandson of Balban, and reigned briefly (1287–90). The site of the city he founded is believed to be where the present-day village of Kilokri is situated.

18 'Nestled in Paradise', the official posthumous title accorded to Humayun.

19 The founder of the Khilji dynasty, Jalal-ud-Din (r. 1290–96).

Din Khilji laid the foundation of another city and built a new fort, which was called Siri.[20]

Sultan Ghiyas-ud-Din Tughlaq[21] laid the foundation of a city and fort called Tughlaqabad in 725 [1324–25]. Ghiyas-ud-Din's older son Muhammad Bin Tughlaq, during his reign, built a new palace and had a grand hall built in it, in the construction of which a thousand painted marble pillars were used. This ruler also built other magnificent buildings.[22]

In 755 [1354–55], Sultan Firoz Shah laid the foundation of Firozabad, diverted the course of the river Jamuna and brought it near the city. At a distance of about 3 *kos* from this city he built another palace with a pillar called the Jahan Numa Minar, which can still be seen at Kotla Firoz Shah and is called 'Firoz Shah ki Lath' by the common people. He also constructed a tunnel through which one could ride from Firozabad to Jahan Numa.[23]

The honourable Syed Khizr Khan, in about 900 [1494–95], after the return of Amir Kabir Taimur Gorkani, the death of Sultan Mahmud and the end of the rule of the Turks,[24] had the fort of Khizrabad built, which is commonly known as Gumti-e-Khizr. Amir Taimur[25] arrived on the tenth day of the month of Jamadi-ul-Awwal, Wednesday, 801 [1398]. He fought with Sultan Mahmud, son of Humayun Khan Iskandar, son of Sultan Muhammad Shah, son of Firoz Shah; and with Sultan Mahmud's *wazir*, Mallu Iqbal Khan. Victorious in this battle, Amir Taimur returned to his homeland. After he left, the building of Khizrabad was constructed.

---

[20] 'Ala-ud-Din Khilji (r. 1296–1316). The remains of Siri can be seen in the area now occupied by Shahpur Jat village and Asian Games Village.

[21] The founder of the Tughlaq dynasty, Ghiyas-ud-Din (r. 1320–25).

[22] Muhammad Tughlaq reigned from 1325 to 1351, and founded the city of Jahanpanah. The so-called palace of a thousand pillars is located at the site known as Bijay Mandal, and close by is the large Begampuri Masjid, the congregational mosque of the city.

[23] The description of these two locations is a bit confusing. In fact, Firoz Shah built the citadel known as Firoz Shah Kotla in the city of Firozabad, and at some distance from this, on the Northern Ridge, he built a hunting lodge called Jahan Numa ('world revealing', because of its location on a height). At each of these locations he installed a stone pillar. These were monolithic Ashokan pillars, dating to the third century BCE, which Firoz Shah had found on his expeditions to Haryana and Meerut, respectively, and had transported to his capital. Though tales of tunnels abound, no concrete evidence of this has come to light. The author mentions the Western Yamuna Canal, built by Firoz Shah.

[24] The date is clearly inaccurate. Khizr Khan, who founded the Syed dynasty in 1414, is said to have established Khizrabad in 1410. No signs of this city, located next to the Yamuna, remain today.

[25] Known to many as Tamerlane.

In 900 [1494–95], Syed Khizr Khan's son Mubarak Shah established the settlement of Mubarakabad. His tomb is close to Safdarjang's tomb near *mauza* Chhatarpur.[26]

Babur gained victory over Ibrahim Lodhi in 930 [1523–24]. Emperor Humayun's date of birth may be derived from this verse: 'Our good fortune rose with the star of Humayun.'[27] [913/1508]

Humayun was first defeated[28] in 954 [1540] at Gaur, that is, Lakhnauti. He met his second defeat on the tenth day of the month of Muharram in 947 [1541] this side of the river Ganga. But the third time he captured Hindustan. The date of his victory is this:

[1]   The Keeper of intellect called for a pleasant temperament. For the art of writing, He called for a creative temperament.

[2]   When he conquered Hindustan, he commanded the date by the sword of Humayun/the auspicious sword. [962/1555]

 In 937 [1530–31], Naseer-ud-Din Humayun had the fort of Inderpat, which was completely deserted, repaired and named it Dinpanah. Today this fort is known as Purana Qila. Some people are of the opinion that Sher Shah also repaired parts of this fort during his reign. Sher Shah's date of death is this:

[1]   Sher Shah established the rule of justice, through which both the lion and the goat came to drink the same water.

[2]   He who left the mortal world, then the wise man said that his date can be gleaned from his death by fire. [952/1545]

---

[26]   Again, this date is wrong; Mubarak Shah Syed ascended the throne in 1421 and is believed to have founded Mubarakabad, of which no evidence survives, in 1433. His tomb is located in present-day Lodi Garden.

[27]   In the verse 'Humayun' means both the name of the emperor and 'auspicious'. The year of Babur's defeat of Ibrahim Lodi is actually 1526. Sangin Beg does not dwell on the Lodi rulers or Babur, the founder of the Mughal dynasty, because they are not associated with any new settlement in Delhi. However, a large number of buildings of the Lodi period can be seen in Delhi.

[28]   He was defeated by Sher Shah Sur, who founded a dynasty that ruled from 1540 to 1556, before Humayun won back his territories.

The second chronogram is this:

Badshah Sher Shah is he who died by fire. [952/1545]

He was an Afghan. He plundered the city of Alai, which was called Siri, and constructed a new city and named it Sher Mandal.[29] This city was near the Purana Qila, but today it is completely deserted. His son Salim Shah built the Salimgarh fort in two years' time at a cost of four lakh rupees, completing it in 953 [1546–47].

The establishment of the *Dar-ul-Khilafa* Shahjahanabad, and the construction of the fort built by Shah Jahan[30]

On the fifth day of the month of Zil-Hajj 1048 [16 April 1639], in the twelfth regnal year of Shah Jahan Badshah-e-Ghazi, orders were given to commence the digging of the foundation of the fort. In the beginning of 1049, on the evening of Friday the ninth of Muharram [12 May 1639], at twelve minutes past five, the time prescribed by astrological calculations, the construction of the foundations of the fort was commenced. The construction of the fort was completed in the twenty-first year of the accession of Shah Jahan. The fort was completed in nine years at a cost of Rs 59,05,000. The details of the expenditure are as follows:

The Royal Palace and the Assembly of the Diwan-e-Khas	2 lakhs
The Hayat Bakhsh garden and the Hammam	6 lakhs
The palaces of the daughter of the emperor, Nawab Jahan Ara Begam, and other royal ladies	7 lakhs
Internal courts of the fort, the royal workshops and other buildings	4 lakhs
The ramparts and the moat	21 lakhs
Wells, stepwells, etc.	95,000

The length of the fort is 1,000 Shahjahani yards and the width 300 yards. The

---

[29] Stones were carried away from the abandoned city of Siri for the construction of his city which was called Shergarh, close to Humayun's Dinpanah. Sher Mandal is actually a building in the Purana Qila.

[30] Sangin Beg takes these details of the construction of the Red Fort from the accounts of the court chroniclers of Shah Jahan's reign.

height of the walls is 25 yards. The length and breadth of the foundations below the ground is 15 yards, and the width above the ground is 10 yards. The total area of the fort is 6,00,000 yards, i.e. twice that of the fort of Agra.

On the twenty-fourth of the month of Rabi'-ul-Awwal 1058 [1648] Shah Jahan entered the fort and his residence through the gate on the riverside, which opens into the royal palace.

On the gateway of the hall of the Diwan-e-Khas is written in gold letters: 'If there is paradise on earth, it is here, it is here, it is here.'[31]

The details of the buildings in the Qil'a-e-Mubarak [Auspicious Fort] are as follows

From the Dehli Gate of the fort where a brass cannon commonly known as Kale Khan is lying, there is the house of Nazir Manzur 'Ali[32] and houses of the descendants of the emperors,[33] a locality that is famous by the name of Naumuhalla. Inside this, in the Asad Burj, is the *mahal* of Mirza Jahangir Bahadur[34] and the residence of Mirza Neeli, the brother of Muhammad Akbar Badshah-e-Ghazi.[35] Here, on the way towards the threshold, is Khawaspura, the *chowk* in front of the palace gate, and the Naqqar Khana. In the *chowk* between the Naqqar Khana and the *chhatta* of the Lahori Gate, the Faiz Nahar flows. Adjoining this *chhatta* is the *haveli* of Nazir Ishrat 'Ali. Over the Lahori Gate is the residence of the commander of the palace guard, Captain MacPherson Bahadur,[36] and the houses of several royal servants and common people. Inside the Naqqar Khana is the Diwan-e-'Am where, during the period from the reign of Shah

---

31 The couplet was composed by the great poet Amir Khusro (1253–1325).

32 The title 'Nazir' signifies a senior eunuch in charge of the royal household.

33 The extended Mughal family lived in the Naumohalla. They included distant cousins and other relatives of the emperor, who were known as the *salatin*.

34 Jahangir was the son of Akbar II, who was on the throne between 1806 and 1837, though as a pensioner of the East India Company. The house in question was probably near Asad Burj, which is a bastion at the south-east angle of the wall of the Red Fort. These and many more buildings inside the fort were demolished by the British after the revolt of 1857.

35 i.e. Akbar II.

36 The British stationed their own troops at the gates of the fort in 1809.

Jahan Badshah-e-Ghazi to that of Hazrat Firdaus Manzil,[37] Shah Alam, the emperors held their court. To the east of this is the *zanana* threshold of the Shah Mahal, which is known as the Deorhi-e-'Adalat.[38] Adjacent to the Diwan-e-'Am is a screen door. Inside this is the open court of the Diwan-e-Khas. In this court is the hall of the Diwan-e-Khas. Here there is also a door that is screened with a red curtain. The courtiers, ministers and servants of the emperor, who are given admittance to the presence to kiss the feet of the 'Shadow of God', present their salutations, compliments and obeisance from this place which is in front of the emperor. Inside this curtain is the exalted *mahal*, the Mussamman Burj, where the emperor sits; the Moti Masjid; the backyard of the *hammam* and the Jama Kun [the place for changing clothes]. Here at present the Heir-Apparent sits. Obviously, this *hammam* is without compare in the world. Here there is the Moti Mahal, the Shah Burj, and the northern and southern open *dalans* [balconies]. Also there is the Hayat Bakhsh garden which is known as Sawan Bhadon. There is a big tank in the middle of it.[39]

In front of the *dalan* of the Moti Mahal too is a marble tank. This is made of a single block of marble and has no joints. In the middle of the Moti Mahal also there is a tank which is made of a single block of stone. On either side of the Moti Mahal flows a

---

37 'Located in Paradise', the title given to Shah 'Alam (r. 1759–1806) posthumously, in the usual style of the Mughal emperors.

38 Visitors to the Red Fort today know this palace better as Rang Mahal or Imtiyaz Mahal.

39 Many of the important buildings described by Sangin Beg still survive, though not their enclosed courtyards. The big tank in the Hayat Bakhsh garden now contains the red sandstone building known as Zafar Mahal, constructed after Sangin Beg's account was penned. The two marble pavilions in the garden are called Sawan and Bhadon, after the rainy months of the year.

python-shaped stream. These tanks and streams are connected to the Hayat Bakhsh garden. The Shah Burj of the Qil'a-e-Mubarak is to the north of this palace. The water of the Faiz Nahar reaches the fort through this tower.[40] In this tower are two tanks. Neither the tongue nor the pen can have the impudence to describe even a little of the exquisiteness of these tanks – especially the tank that is adjacent to the wall of the Shah Burj, which is said to be made of jasper.

In the other part of this garden, which is known as Mahtab Bagh, is the building where holy relics are kept. Here is also the building of the court of justice as well as other buildings.

There is a door to the north of the Diwan-e-'Am. Outside it is the emperor's stable, the Khasah Kalan and Khurd, the path that leads to the door of Mahtab Bagh and the Chobi Masjid [wooden mosque] from where the path leads to Mirza Jahangir's new *haveli*, Chandni Chowk and the houses of the Salatin.[41] To the west of the Diwan-e-'Am is a big gateway, which is known as the gateway of the Naqqar Khana. This is a tall building. Here drums are beaten thrice in the day: morning, evening and at midnight. On Sunday the drums are beaten many times in the day because this day is associated with the Sun.[42] Similarly, on Wednesday the drums are beaten throughout the day as this is the day of the auspicious accession of Hazrat Muhammad Akbar Shah Ghazi, the Caliph of God. Behind Mahtab Bagh is a building of the emperor, residences of Mirza Farhat Bakht, Mirza Tifl, Mirza Mughal Sahib, the *hammam* of the late Mirza Jawan Bakht, the building of the royal arsenal, and the gate next to the Salimgarh bridge. The bridge was built by Emperor Nur-ud-Din Jahangir.[43] Its eastern wall bears the following inscription on the marble:

---

[40] The Moti Mahal no longer exists. The water flowing through the gardens and the palace buildings that were located along the eastern side of the fort was that of the Faiz Nahar, or Nahar-e-Bahisht, a canal built in the fourteenth century by orders of Emperor Firoz Shah Tughlaq, to bring water from the Yamuna to his hunting preserve at Safidon. This was repaired and extended when Shahjahanabad was founded, to supply water to the city as well as the palace.

[41] The structures in this part of the fort were demolished in the second half of the nineteenth century and replaced with barracks.

[42] To the Mughal rulers, as to many ruling powers throughout history, the sun symbolized royalty, and was incorporated in many rituals and depictions. See Harbans Mukhia, *The Mughals of India*, Blackwell Publishing, Oxford, 2005, pp. 47–49.

[43] The Mughal emperor (r. 1605–27).

[1] This bridge was built on the orders of Nur-ud-din Jahangir, the great.

[2] Its year and date, 'Indeed, the right path'. [1031/1621–22]

On the western wall of the bridge the following chronogram is inscribed:

[1] *Allah is great!*
By the order of the king of the seven climes
Eminent is His glory
The emperor of justice and redress
The Opener!
[One of God's names]

[2] *O Nasir!*
Jahangir, Son of Emperor Akbar
The Effulgent One
Whose sword subdues the world
O Thou Life!
[One of God's names]

[3] In Year 17 this bridge in Dehli was constructed
The Coronation
Its description is unsuited to words *of Jahangir*

[4] As for the date of its completion, intelligence says:
Husain
'The Bridge of the Emperor of Dehli, Jahangir'. [1031/1621–22]
The Holy Name

A description of the other particular features and buildings of this paradise-like palace and tall fort

The distinctive features of this magnificent palace and sky-like fort, and its heavenly buildings, are so numerous that lacking in eloquence as I am, I cannot describe them even briefly. I therefore leave the description of these peculiar features to the detailed old books and carry my narrative forward.

From the Dehli Gate of the fort to the Ajmeri Gate of the city wall, that is, to the south-west, first, there is a square in front of the fort. This is called the Chowk-e-Nawab

Sa'dullah Khan.[44] Sa'dullah Khan was the chief minister of Shah Jahan Badshah-e-Ghazi. His name was Mulla Sa'dullah and he belonged to Lahore. In 1050 [1640–41], the fourteenth regnal year of Shah Jahan, he entered the service of the emperor in Lahore. He was exalted by the award of a horse from the special stable of the emperor, and in a year's time he was favoured with a *mansab* of one thousand and the title of Khan.[45] He was also entrusted with the duty of superintendence of the royal household. In Shah Jahan's nineteenth regnal year, on the first day of the month of Jamadi-us-Sani 1055 [1645–46], he was favoured with a special *khil'at*.[46] He was also given the *diwani* of the Khalisa Sharifa[47] in place of Islam Khan, a *mansab* of 4,000 *zat* and 1,000 *sawar*, and a jewelled inkstand. On the twentieth day of the month of Rajab in the same year, he was favoured with complete ministership, a special *khil'at*, a dagger with a jewelled handle. His *mansab* was increased to 5,000 *zat* and an additional 500 *sawar*. After this, in the month of Zil-Hajj in 1058 [1648–49], the twenty-second regnal year of Shah Jahan, Sa'dullah Khan was favoured with a *mansab* of 7,000 and 7,000 *sawar, do aspah* and *sih aspah*. On the twenty-second day of Jamadi-us-Sani 1066 [17 April 1656], the thirtieth regnal year of Shah Jahan, Sa'dullah Khan was afflicted with a painful disease of the intestines and passed away. In the same year, Mir Muhammad Sa'id Mir Jumla Qutb-ul-Mulk,[48] the governor of Hyderabad, came from the Deccan and presented himself to the emperor, and was given the title of Mu'azzam Khan and the position of minister. The period of Sa'dullah Khan's prime ministership was about twelve years. Allah is all-knowing.

Every year *chhadis* of Ghazi Miyan and Madar Sahib are set up in the *chowk* of Sa'dullah Khan, and the people of the city gather here in large numbers.[49]

---

[44] This square was obliterated by the demolitions in the city immediately following the revolt of 1857.

[45] *Mansabdari* was a system by which all officials of the empire were given personal and military ranks, expressed as *zat* (personal) and *sawar* (horse, i.e. cavalrymen). The cavalry ranks were again complicated by the categories *do aspah, sih aspah* – providing for the maintenance of additional cavalrymen.

[46] *Khil'at* usually consisted of a robe, and often other items of clothing and adornment, personally given by the emperor as a mark of favour.

[47] This important position was that of officer in charge of lands reserved as sources of revenue for the Mughal state, as opposed to *jagir* lands which were assigned in lieu of military or other services.

[48] Mir Jumla was a powerful noble in the service of Qutb Shah, ruler of Golconda, who played an important role in the kingdom's conflict with the Mughal empire and eventually came over to the Mughal side.

[49] The festivals of these two popular saints were celebrated with the setting up of *chhadis* (standards).

The description of the area surrounding this *chowk* is as follows

Towards the east is Rajghat and thereabouts; to the west is Khas Bazar; towards the north the Lahori Gate of the Qil'a-e-Mubarak, Nigambodh and other areas; to the south is the Sunehri Masjid of Nawab Bahadur Khan, the Akbarabadi Masjid, Kashmiri Katra, the way to the Dehli Gate and other areas. To the east of this *chowk* is the Mohalla-e-Kashti Banan,[50] the *haveli* of Asad 'Ali Hazari, Baghichah-e-Payeen, the *khidki* of the Pan Chakki and the city's Rajghat Gate.[51] Towards the Khas Chowk is the bazar of handicraftsmen, shops and the way to the Khanam's Bazar. After this is the *haveli* of 'Abdur Rasul Khan, the superintendent of the Shahi Abdar, the Bulaqi Begam street,[52] houses of the populace, shops of pedlars, and the *mazar* complex of Shah Sarmad.[53] He was killed during the reign of Sultan 'Alamgir Aurangzeb at a time when he was lost in divine meditation. Adjoining this is the *mazar* of Shah Hare Bhare Darvesh[54] and the building of the royal Cheeni Khana,[55] which is located below the Jama Masjid.

The inscriptions of the Jama Masjid of the *Dar-ul-Khilafa* Shahjahanabad

Emperor Shah Jahan had this mosque constructed. It has eleven doors on the outside and seven doors towards the inside. Inside on the head of the *mihrab*, facing the large entrance at the place for the *imam* to stand, the following inscription is engraved in Sulus script:[56]

> There is a mosque whose foundation was laid from the first day on piety; it is more worthy of the standing forth (for prayer) therein. In it are men who love to be purified; and Allah loveth those who make themselves pure. [9:108]

---

[50] Literally, the neighbourhood of boat-makers.

[51] The city wall had a number of openings, big and small. Here Sangin Beg mentions two, both on the eastern side. The *khidki* was a small doorway named after a water-mill or *pan chakki*, and the Rajghat Gate was located just south of the fort.

[52] Bulaaqi Begam was the daughter of Danial, son of Akbar. She was thus the aunt of Shah Jahan.

[53] Also known as Sarmad Shaheed ('martyr'), Sarmad was an Armenian Jew who adopted Islam and an extremely ascetic lifestyle. Shah Jahan's son Dara Shukoh had a reverence for Sarmad, and this, together with his orthodoxy, probably led Aurangzeb to order his execution.

[54] Not much is known about this saint, whose disciple was Sarmad. Their shrines are next to each other.

[55] A place where china was kept.

[56] An elegant Arabic script.

In the name of Allah, Most Gracious, Most Merciful.

Say: 'O my Servants who have transgressed against their souls! Despair not of the Mercy of Allah: for Allah forgives all sins: for He is Oft-Forgiving, Most Merciful.'
[39:53]

In both the internal and outer *dalans* of the mosque the marble prayer carpets number 859. These are the inscriptions over the doorways in Naskh script:

On the first arch

By the order of the Emperor of the world; King of the earth and the age; Lord of the world; conqueror of kingdoms; master of the world; powerful as the sky; founder of the laws of justice and administration; strengthener of the pillars of state and wealth; well-knowing; of exalted nature; whose commands are like the decree of fate, and position like that of Providence; of happy intellect and auspicious appearance; fortunate and lucky; having grandeur like the firmament, soldiers (as numerous) as stars; glory like the sun and the court (as spacious) as the sky.

On the second arch

The manifestation of the Almighty's power; the recipient of unlimited blessings; the proclaimer of the great word of God; the promulgator of the bright faith of Hanifa; the asylum of princes and kings; the deputy of God on earth; the just and great king; the great and glorious Lord Abul Muzaffar Shihab-ud-Din Muhammad Sahib Qiran-e-Sani [second Lord of the Happy Conjunction][57] Shah Jahan Badshah-e-Ghazi [the king and champion of faith], may the flags of his kingdom ever remain victorious, and the enemies of his Majesty subdued, whose eye of God-seeing perception is lighted up by the radiance of the lights of guidance of 'Verily he populates mosques of God';

On the third arch

Who believes in God and the last day, and the mirror of whose truth-adopting conscience has received light from the flame of the lamp of the tradition, 'The places most loved by God are mosques'; this mosque with its foundation (as firm) as a mountain of the noble [verse] 'Verily the mosque founded on piety', and the clear [verse] 'The mountains were cast into the earth in order to make it firm' for the inscription of its strong hall; whose sky-like pinnacle and dome have gone beyond the folds of the firmament, and the cornice of whose sky-like vaults has reached the height of Saturn;

On the fourth arch

[1] If you want to know what the vault and cupola of its prayer chamber are like, nothing can be said except (that they resemble) the Milky Way and sky.

[2] The dome would have been matchless had the firmament not been its equal, the vault would have been unique had the Milky Way not been its pair.

The brilliance of the ornament of whose world-showing arch gives light to the lamps of heaven [i.e. stars]; and the reflection of the pinnacle of whose world-adorning dome increases the height of the chandelier of Paradise; whose marble pulpit, like the rock of Solomon's temple, is a ladder to;

---

[57] Taimur was referred to as Sahib Qiran, 'Lord of the Happy Conjunction', on account of his birth having taken place at the time of an auspicious conjunction of planets. His descendant Shah Jahan, having been born under similar astrological circumstances, was known as Sahib Qiran-e-sani, Second Lord of the Happy Conjunction.

On the fifth arch

The point 'Qaba qausaini aw adna' [close proximity between the Prophet and God]; whose grace-spreading *mihrab*, like the true and broad-foreheaded dawn, give the good news, 'Verily there has come to them from their God the right path'; whose doors, which are the resort of mercy, have brought to the hearing of the great and small the announcement, 'And God invites to the abode of peace'; whose *minars*, which are the orbits of heavens, have sent the call, '(God) will compensate those who do good with goodness' beyond the nine folds of the blue-coloured dome [the sky]; whose lofty and polished roof is the pleasure-ground of the spirits of the celestial sphere;

On the sixth arch

This is an intermediate entrance and is larger than two adjacent doorways. On both corners of its *mihrab* the *tughra* of 'Ya Hadi' [O Guide!] is inscribed in the following manner:

يا هادى

يا هادى   يا هادى

يا هادى

On the seventh arch

Whose spacious and pleasant courtyard is the place of worship of the pure-born of the terrestrial and populated world, and the favourable, refreshing, good and soul-strengthening air thereof resembles [the breeze of] the garden of Paradise; the sweetness of the pure water of whose pleasing and purifying tank represents the spring of Salsabil [a spring in Paradise], on Friday, the tenth of the month of Shawwal of the year one thousand and sixty, corresponding to the fourth year of the third cycle of the auspicious reign, at the propitious moment;

On the eighth arch

And the fortunate time obtained the wealth of foundation and ornament of stability; and during the period of six years, with the efficient exertions and skilful workmen, with the great application and devotion of respectable superintendents, with the hearty efforts of sagacious and wise masters, and with the great exertions of apt-handed and skilled artificers at a cost of ten lakhs of rupees, obtained the form of completion and the feature of finish. Soon after its completion, on the day of *Id-i-Fitr;*

On the ninth arch

It was adorned and embellished by the magnificence of the holiest steps of the king, the shadow of God, pure-intentioned and God-knowing; and on the day of *Id-i-Azha* it became the resort of crowds of people, by his [the King's] saying the *Id* prayers and discharging the exercises of Islam as [is done] in the Masjid-ul-Haram [Ka'ba], and blessed the foundations of Islam and faith with firmness and strength. To those who have made the tour of the inhabited fourth portion [of the globe] and the travellers [traversing] mountains and woods, an adorned building of such loftiness and strength has never been reflected in the mirror of their sight.

On the tenth arch

And the looking-glass of their imagination, nor to the relaters of the events of the age and the careful students of prose and poetry, who are the biographers of the important personages of the country and kingdom, and are the connoisseurs of the persons of might and power, has a lofty edifice of such grandeur and magnificence been brought to the tongue of their pen and the pen of their tongue. May the builder of the mansion of life and the designer of high and low places keeping this exalted building firm, which is like the pupil of the eye of sight, and the embellisher of the workhouse of creation;

On the eleventh arch

Continue the sound of the repeaters of the praises of God on a rosary, in it, giving grace to the noise of the assembly of God-praising angels, and the melodious voice of the readers of the Muhammadan creed and the name of God, in it, increasing joy of the congregations of recluse angels of the highest order; and decorate the heads of the pulpits of the inhabited world with the *khutba* of the eternity-adorning reign of this king who is an administrator of justice and a cherisher of faith, and by the blessings of whose august and holy person the doors of peace and security have been opened for the worlds, for the sake of God and His people. Written by Nurullah Ahmad.[58]

Towards the northern gate of the mosque, within an enclosure, are some relics of the Prophet. On the door of this red sandstone screen enclosure, a chronogram is engraved which gives the date 1164 [1750–51], thus:

[1] In front of the blessed relics of the chief of the last age [the Prophet Muhammad] during the time of Shah 'Alamgir, the king of the world,

[2] With greatness a wall of red stone was built, with a true heart, by the faithful slave Ilmas Khan.

[3] When Mir asked thought and intelligence for the year of its erection, an invisible voice replied, 'He has opened for himself the doors of Paradise'.[59]

In the middle of the court of the mosque is a tank. In its western corner, on the northern side, in a space large enough for a man to sit, is a railing with this inscription:

Kausar [name of a spring in Paradise] of Muhammad, the messenger of God

[1] Saints and the people of God have seen the Prophet here; it is proper if this stone should also become a place of pilgrimage.

[2] The year of its construction, the invisible voice said with praise and applause, 'The enclosure of the seat of the messenger of God'.

The founder of the place of respect, Muhammad Tahsin, the Royal Eunuch, who prays for blessings.[60] [1180/1766–67]

Within the court, in front of the eastern *dalan* of the mosque, is a sundial to tell the time. There is an iron nail fixed on it.

---

[58] The translation of the inscription is taken from Zafar Hasan, Vol. I, pp. 143–45. The calligraphy was the work of Nurullah Ahmad, son of Ustad Ahmad, the architect of the Red Fort.

[59] Ibid., p. 146.

[60] Ibid., p. 147.

On all sides in the *dalans* there are ten *hujras* [cells]. The number of steps on three sides of the mosque are as follows: to the east thirty-five; to the north thirty-nine; and to the south thirty-three. On the eastern steps, every day in the evening in every season, pigeons and all sorts of animals are sold for enthusiasts and children. Under the northern steps, in the evening a *dastango* comes and tells his stories. On the southern steps, books, arms and all sorts of other things are sold. Behind the mosque in the west, there are shops of sellers of *dal*, the *kothi* of vendors of intoxicants like opium, and shops of grinders of flour, and also the bazar famous by the name of Chawri.

To the north of Chawri Bazar is the building of the Dar-ush-Shifa.[61] Emperor Shah Jahan had this built for ill travellers and students. Here they were given medical treatment and were healed. Here is the doorway of the *haveli* of Bahadur 'Ali Khan, the way to the doorway of Chhatta Shah Nizam-ud-Din,[62] his *havelis*, the Mohalla Roshanpura, and stable of A'zam-ud-Daulah Mu'in-ul-Mulk Nawab Muhammad Amir Khan Bahadur. Here there is a banyan tree known by the name of Barh Shah Bola. Shah Bola was a *darvesh* in the time of Shah Jahan. His grave is also in this place. The Kucha-e-Naiwarah is also here.[63] From this *kucha* to Kucha-e-Charkhewalan are shops of braziers where utensils of copper and brass are sold. In the midst of the bazar there is a brackish well. In the bazar are also the *havelis* of Qutbi Begam and Hakim Baqa,[64] and the building of the Ilahabad Police Chowki. Here in the middle of the bazar is the Hauz Qazi. Here there are shops of *sarkiwalas* [makers of reed matting]. Behind the *havelis* of Nawab Turk Jang[65] and Qutbi Begam there is a *kucha* and the *gali* [street] of Shah Tara.[66] Here there are houses of the populace. From here to the Ajmeri Gate are the shops of cobblers who make shoes. Connected to Ajmeri Gate are the path of the city wall and the barracks of the gunners.

---

[61] 'Place of healing'.

[62] Shah Nizam-ud-Din, also called Shahji, was a holy man who enjoyed the confidence of Shah 'Alam II, and was also the governor of Delhi during 1789–96 and 1798–1801, appointed by the Maratha chief Mahadji Sindhia who controlled Delhi at the time.

[63] Literally, the street of barbers.

[64] Hakim Baqa was a renowned practitioner of Unani medicine in the eighteenth century.

[65] See note 74 below.

[66] Shah Tara was the daughter of Qamar-ud-Din Khan, who was appointed the *wazir* or minister by the Mughal emperor Muhammad Shah in 1724. Qamar-ud-Din Khan died in 1748. Shah Tara built a large mansion, and the street on which it was located came to be known after her.

From Chawri Bazar towards Ajmeri Gate in the south, first, is located the building of the Dar-ul-Baqa. This was built by Shah Jahan Badshah-e-Ghazi for the distribution of charity and offerings among religious mendicants, the indigent and needy travellers. After this comes the Chitla Darwaza where there are houses of the common people. Another path leads from here to the *haveli* of Mir Jhuma, the uncle of Emperor Muhammad Akbar Shah Ghazi.

From the Chitla Darwaza begin the shops of artisans and *kaghazis* [sellers of paper?], the Kucha Mir 'Ashiq and Kucha Batashewalan. Towards the *haveli* of Raja Kedarnath[67] there is a *gali* [street] in which there are shops of grocers and ironsmiths, and the Kucha Murghan. The other end of this opens into the Imli ka Mohalla. From here to the aforementioned Hauz Qazi there is the building of the soldiers of Ilahabad Police Chowki, the *katra* of Punjabi *garibans* [coachmen], the *haveli* of Muhammad Shah's *wazir* Nawab Qamar-ud-Din Khan,[68] the building of the Karor ki Kachehri. Here is also the Mohalla Jatwarah.[69] Near the Ajmeri Gate of the city, the mosque of Khalilullah Khan is located. It bears towards its northern side the chronogram:

[1] What a beautiful mosque, which by reason of its eminence became a place of worship for a beggar and an emperor.

[2] Its foundation was laid in the reign of 'Alamgir, through the favour of the Prophet, the messenger of God.

[3] The invisible crier spake the date of this sanctuary: 'Khalilullah built a Ka'ba'.[70]
[1080 /1669–70]

To the north of Hauz Qazi are: the shop of a *rewdiwala*, the *haveli* of Raja Sedh Mal, the *haveli* of Raja Jai Singh, the *haveli* of the late Nawab Turk Jang Badal Beg Khan,[71] and the gateway of the *haveli* of Hafiz 'Abdur Rahman Khan. Hafiz 'Abdur Rahman Khan

---

[67] A functionary in the employment of Akbar II.

[68] Qamar-ud-Din Khan is better known by his title I'timad-ud-Daulah. He rose in position steadily from the last years of Aurangzeb's reign, becoming Muhammad Shah's prime minister in 1724. He died in 1748.

[69] Literally, the neighbourhood of Jats.

[70] Zafar Hasan, Vol. I, p. 79.

[71] Badal Beg Khan was a *risaldar*, commander of a military troop, in the second half of the eighteenth century.

is the *mukhtar-e-sarkar*[72] of the emperor's brother, Mirza Neeli. Near this *haveli* is the house of Bajna *tawaif* [courtesan]. During the first ten days of Muharram she prepares an idol of Deo and puts it up at her door. On the same street are shops of makers of copper vessels and the *haveli* of the late Shadil Khan, where currently Mirza Mughal Beg lives.[73] After this is the house of Nurullah Khan and the Kucha Pandit. In Kucha Pandit are the *haveli* of Sar Buland Khan[74] and Shah Pasand Khan, and the houses of Naina Beg Khan and other common people. From here one street leads to Kucha-e-Shah Tara, which has been mentioned earlier.

Next to the Kucha Pandit are the mosque and house of the late Miyan Jan Sahib. This locality also has shops of bangle-makers, the Hijron ka Katra, Sabz Masjid and a well, and Adina Beg's *katra*. The Sabz Masjid bears this chronogram:

[1]   Adina Beg, who is a Khan of exalted rank, and whom God has given considerable resources to do good deeds,

[2]   Built a mosque, like the garden of Paradise, and such that it will be justifiable if it were called 'Ka'ba' in praise.

[3]   See that the writing of its inscription says, the date of is erection is 'come to the house of religion'.[75] [1196 /1781–81]

In front of this is the house of Nawab Fatehullah Beg Khan, and towards the *haveli* of the late Nawab Sohrab Jang Qasim Khan[76] is the gateway of a lane. In this lane are located, first, the *haveli* and mosque of Muhammad Khan Karora,[77] the *haveli* and

---

72 This means chief agent or functionary.

73 Shadil Khan was a military captain during the reign of 'Alamgir II (r. 1754–59). The later occupant of the *haveli*, Mirza Mughal Beg, was a Mughal prince.

74 Sar Buland Khan was the governor of the provinces of Bihar and Gujarat during the reigns of Farrukhsiyar (r. 1713–19) and Muhammad Shah (r. 1719–48).

75 Zafar Hasan, Vol. I, p. 96. Adina Beg was a noble during the reigns of Muhammad Shah and his son Ahmad Shah (r. 1748–54). He died in 1756, which puts in question the date in the mosque's inscription.

76 Qasim Jan, whose father came from Bukhara, rose to the high position of deputy chief minister during the reign of Shah 'Alam II.

77 Muhammad Khan Karora was a tax official when Akbar II was on the throne.

stable building of the deceased Nawab, the house of Teerandaz Khan, the *haveli* of Nawab Ahmad Bakhsh Khan,[78] and the Diwan Khana [house] of Faizullah Beg Khan.[79] Here is also a mosque built by the late Khan, on the northern side of which is inscribed the chronogram:

[1] The erection of this mosque which is like a garden of Paradise was effected by the hands of Qasim Khan.

[2] A well which is like Zamzam and has sweet water he dedicated, as well as four shops.

[3] When he asked Rafi' its date, he replied, 'Suhrab Jang Qasim Khan'.[80] [1193 /1779]

This lane goes on to Ballimaran. After the *haveli* of Nawab Fatehullah Beg Khan, who has been mentioned before, is the mosque of Khalifa Bakhshu, may Allah's blessing be upon him; Kucha Khidki Faraash Khana;[81] Mohalla Roodgaran;[82] the houses of Mir Jumla, the house of Khwaja Bhikari Sahib, and the *haveli* of Kakwan Sahib.

After the mosque of Khalifa Bakhshu are shops of ironsmiths and the house of Teerandaz Khan. Here, in the middle of the market, is a well which is famous as the Lal Kuan. Near this is the Katra Shaikh Chand where there are houses of the common people. Here is the *haveli* of Mir Jumla, the building of the police *chowki* of Qasim Khan and Kucha Samosa,[83] the other end of which goes towards the Khidki Farash Khana. In this *kucha* are the houses of Hakim Zakaullah Khan[84] and others, and a

---

[78] Ahmad Bakhsh Khan was a military commander who was rewarded for his services to the East India Company in 1803 with two *jagirs*: Loharu and Firozpur Jhirka. His eldest son, Shams-ud-Din Khan, was found guilty of a conspiracy to murder William Fraser, the Resident at Delhi, and was executed in 1835.

[79] Son of Qasim Jan.

[80] Zafar Hasan, Vol. I, p. 112.

[81] *Farash Khana* literally means a room where furniture or lumber is kept. This *khidki* or gate in the city wall was probably next to some such building.

[82] *Roodgaran* are workers manufacturing gut-strings for uses such as sewing leather and for bow-strings.

[83] *Samosa* literally means triangle, and thus also the popular triangle-shaped fried snack. In this context it is hard to say what it refers to.

[84] A well-known practitioner and teacher of Unani medicine.

haveli constructed by Nawab Najaf Khan,[85] known as the *haveli* of Nazir Latafat 'Ali Khan. Beside it are houses of the common people; of Maulvi Qutb-ud-Din Sahib, son of the excellent gentleman, the pride of knowledge, leader of saints, Maulvi Fakhr-ud-Din Sahib,[86] may the mercy of Allah be upon him; and of Mir Hamid 'Ali Sahib Patabaz.[87] Outside the above-mentioned *kucha*, near the building of the soldiers of the late Qasim Khan, is the shop of a flower-seller. Here also sit the *dalals* [salesmen] of chabuk sawars. After this, towards the Fatehpuri Masjid is a street in which are located Katra Gondi,[88] Katra Badiyan, i.e. of those who make *badis*,[89] Kalal Khana,[90] and *havelis* of the populace. After this is the *haveli* of Shah Nawaz Khan[91] and Masjid Tahawwur Khan. On the door of this mosque is inscribed:

> Whoever came with inclination and belief [to the mosque] evening and morning, he was accosted by the house from invisibility: 'come and acquire grace'.

On the central arch is inscribed this chronogram:

[1] In the reign of Muhammad Shah, Tahawwur Shah of Tashkand built the mosque with divine guidance.

[2] It was one thousand one hundred and forty when this good building was completed with happiness by the exertions of the Khan of exalted position.[92]

After this are the bazars of Khari Baoli and Naya Bans. In Khari Baoli there is a *baoli* and a mosque. On the door of the *baoli* this inscription in Naskh script is engraved:

---

[85] Najaf Khan, who died in 1782, was a prominent nobleman of the reign of Shah 'Alam II. He founded the village of Najafgarh in Delhi.

[86] A revered Sufi saint who died in 1785.

[87] *Patta* is a long, double-edged sword and *pattebaz* are those who are skilled in its use. See Mitra Chenoy, *Shahjahanabad*, pp. 183–84.

[88] *Gond* is edible gum.

[89] Spicy, small, dried lentil cakes.

[90] Literally, a place where arrack, an alchoholic spirit, is sold.

[91] Possibly the same person who was a nobleman at Shah 'Alam II's court and authored a history of Delhi.

[92] Zafar Hasan, Vol. I, p. 99. The year 1140 *Hijri* corresponds to 1727–28. Tahawwur Khan was the *zamindar* of Shahjahanpur.

Oh Allah

There is no God but Allah, and Muhammad is His Messenger.

O Allah

On the inside of the door of the *baoli* is written. in Sulus [script]:

> In the name of Allah, Most Gracious, Most Merciful.
> By the Lord's help everything comes to be, this *baoli* and well in the month of
> Ramzan 958 *Hijri* through the spirit of Muhammad-e-Mustafa, the Messenger
> of the *dargah* of God, in the reign of Islam Shah the Just, son of Sher Shah, was
> constructed by Khwaja 'Imadul Mulk alias 'Abdullah, servant of the Bringer of Faith,
> hopeful of His beneficence and mercy. [958/1551]

On the wall next to the southern doorways, on the second level of the *baoli*, after
eleven steps, in the same Sulus script, this writing is engraved on the marble:

> In the name of Allah, Most Gracious, Most Merciful.
> In the times of the Sultan of Sultans, Abul Muzaffar Islam Shah, son of Sher
> Shah Sultan, may Allah perpetuate his reign, this well was constructed through
> the mercy of Allah and the spirit of the Messenger of Allah by 'Imadul Mulk alias
> Khwaja 'Abdullah in the year 952 [1545].

The same inscription is also engraved on the western and eastern walls of the *baoli*.

Havelis of the populace, shops of handicraftsmen, *rewdiwalas* and *batashewalas*
are located here.

A description of the streets on either side to the south of Hauz Qazi towards Turkman Gate

First of all, the shop of a *halwa'i* [sweets-seller], the *gali* [street] of Imli Bazar, Kucha
Pati Ram, the *bangla* of Hafiz Fida, Kucha Murghan, houses of the people, houses
of Kashmiri Pandits, Dodhadhari ki Haveli, the house of the *tehsildar* of Palam, Lala
Gulab Rai Pandit, Kucha Mai Das, and the Than-e-Panj Piran are located here.

There is another lane here which goes towards Kucha Pati Ram. Besides this there is another *kucha* which goes towards the city wall and is called Kucha Shidi Qasim. In this *kucha* are the residences of Govardhan Kashmiri and Mir Khan Tundah who is without equal in singing and dancing. Here are the *havelis* of Mirza Fatehullah Beg and Maulvi Fateh 'Ali Sahib Jagirdar, and houses of the common people. Here lie the well of Naurang Rai and the *havelis* of the Baniyas. There is a lane that goes towards the city wall, the houses and property of tanners or leather workers. There is the garden of Tansukh Rai Kaghazi, the *hauz* of Nawab Muzaffar Khan[93] and houses of the populace

From the above-mentioned Than-e-Panj Piran
Haveli Lala Basanti Ram, Haveli Sada Sukh Pandit, Bazar Sita Ram and Jani Khan ka Katra where the common people live. Next to this, towards Chhatta Shah Haji,[94] is a

kucha. After this are two streets. One leads to Mohalla Chudigaran[95] and another towards Sital Das's *hammam*. Sital Das is a person from the time of Shah 'Alam. Here there is the *haveli* of Rai Shambhu Nath, the stable of Murtaza Khan, the *haveli* of Raja Kedar Nath, Gadibanon[96] ka Katra and some brackish wells. The other street goes towards the *bangla* of Shidi Faulad Khan,[97] Kucha-e-Imam and houses of the common people.

From the Katra of Jani Khan there emerge three streets. On one there is the rear of the Kali Masjid, the *hauz* of Muzaffar Khan, and the territory of the *jhilli* makers[98] and other artisans. At this junction of three streets is the *haveli* of Mir Mirza, at the door of which is the shop of Samad Jeo goldsmith who is from Khitta. Here there is

---

93 Muzaffar Khan was a noble during the reigns of Jahangir and Shah Jahan.

94 Shah Haji was a trusted employee of Akbar II, and was also deputed to Calcutta in 1808 to lay before the government of the East India Company, the emperor's claims to an increased allowance and the right to appoint his successor. A few years earlier, in 1797–88, he had also briefly served as the Maratha's governor in Delhi.

95 Literally, the neighbourhood of bangle-makers.

96 *Gadiban* are coachmen.

97 Shidi Faulad was a very corrupt *kotwal* of Delhi in the mid-eighteenth century.

98 i.e. makers of parchment.

the house and mosque of the descendant of Sayyid Hasan Rasul Numa,[99] the late Mir 'Ali Naqi Sahib. Then there are the lanes going towards Bhojla Pahadi and Mohalla Bulbuli Khana. Here there is the house of Mirza Jabbar Beg Khan, the *darogha* of the royal arsenal, and those of the Kashmiri Pandits, the *haveli* of Govardhan Das, the *vakil* of Nawab Ahmad Bakhsh Khan, and the *haveli* of 'Azizullah Khan,[100] and houses of the common people. In front of the entrance to this *mohalla* is the mosque of Shah Hussain Wa'iz. On its western door is inscribed:

> When this big house was built and decorated for Hazrat Shah Husain, the foundation of the *madarsa* and *masjid* was laid. [1148/1753]

Near the mosque is the entrance to the tomb of the ex-*subahdar* of the *Dar-ul-Khilafa*, Shah Haji Beg Sahib. After this, towards the hill, are the *havelis* of Hasan 'Ali Khan alias Miyan Husnu and Mirza Mir Fateh 'Ali Shah Sahib, the house of Roshan the cobbler, and the way to Chhatta Me'maran.[101] There are also the *havelis* of Maulvi Muhammad Jan and Hafiz Khairati Sahib, and other houses belonging to the common people.

On the hill from close to Mir 'Ali Naqi's house a third street goes towards Turkman Gate. In the west, towards the southern bazar, is the Kali Masjid, which was constructed before the establishment of the *Dar-ul-Khilafa*, in the reign of Emperor Firoz Shah. Its steps number thirty-two and its domes thirty-four. In the courtyard are two graves. One is Khan-e-Jahan's and the other is his mother's. This mosque was built by Khan-e-Jahan. He had seven mosques built. These mosques will be mentioned at the appropriate places. The common people call this mosque 'Kali Masjid' but its real name is Kalan Masjid. Because of its age its colour has changed. On the entrance of this mosque is written:

> In the name of Allah, Most merciful, Most compassionate. By the grace and kindness of the Creator, in the reign and sovereignty of the religious king, strong by the help of the merciful, Abul Muzaffar Firoz Shah Sultan, may his kingdom be

---

[99] Syed Hasan Rasul Numa was a Sufi saint of the Qadri order; he died in 1692.

[100] Possibly the same 'Azizullah Khan who was a nobleman at the court of Aurangzeb.

[101] *Me'mar* means architect.

perpetuated, this mosque was built by the son of the slave of the threshold, Junan Shah Maqbul entitled Khan Jahan son of Khan Jahan, may God be merciful to that slave. Anyone coming to the mosque should pray for the benefit of the king of the Muslims and recite the *Fatiha* and the *Ikhlas* for this slave, and may God forgive that slave. In honour of the Prophet and his posterity this mosque was finished on the tenth Jamadi-ul-Akhir of the year 789 [1387].[102]

After this is located the *dargah* of Hazrat Shams-ul-'Arifin Shah Turkman Bayabani. He died on the twenty-fourth of Rajab, 937 [1531].[103] In this area are the houses of Sayyid Nur 'Ali Khan and others. Muzaffar Khan's *hauz*, the building of the Police Chowki of Turkman Gate, the houses of the soldiers of this *chowki*, are all located here. Next to this is the property of shepherds and others. Near the Turkman Gate is an old mosque which has an inscription in the Naskh script on its front:

> In the name of Allah, Most Gracious, Most Merciful. There is no God but Allah, and Muhammad is His Messenger.
> The building of the mosque of Salih Bahadur Ibn Husain [is] in the reign of Sultan 'Alamgir in the year 1087 *Hijri* [1676–77].

After this is the *haveli* of the late Nawab Sulaiman Khan. These days he is called 'Mir Bhikari'. Here there is the Turkman Gate, the houses of the soldiers posted at it and the houses of the artillery men.

Below the southern steps of the Jama Masjid

Here lies a street with the shops of pedlars, Kewal Banswala,[104] shoe-sellers, the turban-sellers Fateh Ji and Karim Ji, other craftsmen, and the Imam ka Kucha. Here is the *haveli* of Shaikh Manglu and the residences of other common people. Here is also

---

[102] Zafar Hasan, Vol. I, p. 70. Khan-e-Jahan 'Tilangani' was the prime minister of Firoz Shah Tughlaq, a post inherited by his son Junan Shah Maqbul. The mosque is no longer black, having been painted and tiled.

[103] The date of death is inaccurate. Shah Turkman was a Sufi saint of the Suhrawardi order who died in 1240. The shrine therefore precedes the foundation of Shahjahanabad by several centuries. The Turkman Gate of the city was named after this landmark.

[104] *Banswala* means seller of bamboo.

the Matia Mahal, where there are houses of common people and the *haveli* of the late Nawab Ahmad 'Ali Khan. In front of Matia Mahal is the doorway of a big *haveli*. After this is located the *haveli* of Hazara Beg and the *bangla* of Shidi Faulad Khan. Shidi Faulad Khan was the *kotwal* of the city in the time of Emperor Muhammad Shah. In front of this is the *haveli* of 'Azizabadi Begam and a street towards the Mohalla Bhojla Pahadi.

From here a street leads to Chhatta Shahji and other places. Here there is the building of the Police Chowki of Bhojla Pahad. Behind the police building are the houses of Faizu Rakabdar [riding attendant], soldiers of the *thana* and those belonging to Nawab Murtaza Khan, as well as the shops of artisans. Here, in the bazar, is a junction of three streets. One street from here goes towards Turkman Gate. At the head of this is a grave known as Chitli Qabr. Next to this grave is Kucha Pahadi, on which are located the *havelis* of masons and other common people. From here one street goes towards Kucha Bulbuli Khana and the grave of Mir Fateh 'Ali Shah deceased. In this *kucha* is the house of Mir Muhammadi Sahib.[105] Near this is a mosque, the shops of craftsmen and another path leading to the hill. Here are the *havelis* of Mir Hashim Sahib and the mosque of Hakim Sayyid Qudratullah Khan Sahib.[106] On the door of this mosque is written:

> This attractive and beautiful structure was built twice. About its year, it is said that this mosque is filled with the light of God. [1208/1794–95]

Near this mosque is the Chhatta-e-Momgaran[107] and the house of Miyan Afaq Sahib Pirzadah. Here is another *haveli* of Murtaza Khan and the Diwan Khana of the said Hakim Sahib, over the door of which is inscribed:

> *Dar-ush-Shifa [The Hall of Healing]*
> O Allah.
> Make this place of healing a place of the healing of faith as well.
> O Muhammad.

---

105 A Sufi revered especially by members of the Mughal royal family; he died in 1826–27.

106 A practising *hakim* as well as a poet who wrote under the pen-name 'Qasim'; he died around 1830.

107 *Momgaran* means wax workers.

Here is the house of Shah Nizam 'Ali Sahib and the grave of Mirza Jan-e-Janan Sahib, may God's mercy be upon him, who bears the *takhallus* [pen-name] 'Mazhar'.[108] The following *qit'a* [couplet sequence] is inscribed on the grave of Mazhar Jan-e-Janan:

[1] O Mazhar! Where are you that in search of you, the flower, its scent and colour are separate.

[2] And the pure pearl, around whom, the moon and the sun and the sky revolve.

After this is the *dugdugi* (*khidki*) of Shah Kallan and his house. In this building are *dalans* with three doors, and there are two or three graves inside. Near this are the *havelis* of Hakim Qudratullah Khan, Hakim 'Izzatullah Khan[109] and other common people. Here is also the street that leads to the graveyard of Hazrat Shams-ul-'Arifin Turkman Bayabani. After this are located the *havelis* of the common people and Mohalla Kalyanpura, the other end of which goes towards Ganj Nawab Mir Khan. Next to Mohalla Naughara, towards the above-mentioned residences of shepherds, there is a *kucha* and a way to the Turkman Gate, which has been mentioned earlier.

On the other street from Chitli Qabr to Dehli Gate, first comes the *haveli* of A'zam Khan and many houses of the common people. Here lie the property of shoemakers, the Mandi Charbina,[110] the *haveli* of Kallu the Khawas [favourite attendant] of Hazrat Firdaus Manzil [Shah 'Alam], the residence and the building of the *madarsa* of Maulvi Shah 'Abdul 'Aziz Sahib,[111] the mosque of Shahji Sahib, the way to the residences of the needle-makers and others, and the Kucha Chelan. From here, a street leads to the *haveli* of the late Nawab Mehdi Quli Khan,[112] where Dabir-ud-Daulah Khwaja Farid Khan[113] and Munshi Khalilullah Khan live. Near this street are the houses of Khwaja Mir

---

[108] Mirza Mazhar was a Sufi of the Naqshbandi order and a poet; he died in 1781.

[109] Hakim 'Izzatullah Khan was the son of Qudratullah Khan; he died in 1840.

[110] Literally, mart for grease or tallow.

[111] Shah 'Abdul 'Aziz (1745–1823), the son of Shah Waliullah, was a great Islamic scholar.

[112] A noble of the late eighteenth century.

[113] The maternal grandfather of Sayyid Ahmad Khan, Khwaja Farid worked for some time with the East India Company and later for Akbar II.

Dard Sahib[114] and 'Umar Khan Barhmuchh, and the *haveli* of Hakim Sana'ullah Khan.[115]

After this are the *haveli* and mosque of Namdar Khan and Kamdar Khan, and the houses of 'Abd-ur-Rasul Khan and other people. There is a lane that leads to the Kalan Mahal, popularly known as 'Kala Mahal'. This is the property of Nawab Faiz Muhammad Khan Bahadur.[116] Here is also the house of Faiz Talab Khan,[117] the Rang Mahal and other buildings, the *zanana* buildings, and a new mosque. The other end of this lane leads towards the Dehli Gate.

In Kalan Mahal are located the houses of Ghulam Ahmad Khan, the ex-*kotwal*, and others. From here as well a street leads to the Dehli Gate. Towards the north of Kalan Mahal is the old *madarsa* of Shah 'Abdul 'Aziz and the house of Mir Safdar 'Ali Jaffar.

After this, behind the buildings of Matia Mahal and near the Kucha-e-Chelan, is the bazar of the late Nawab Mir Khan Chaghta who was among the very high nobles of Emperor Muhammad Shah. In this locality, the *ganj* of the said Nawab, Nawab Qalandar 'Ali Khan's *havelis*,[118] a garden and Qassabpura are located.[119] After this is the city wall and the Khidki Mir Khan, which is currently closed.

In this bazar is the *tiraha* of Nawab Bairam Khan. From here one street leads to the above-mentioned Nawab Mehdi Quli Khan's *haveli*, where there are two streets. One goes towards Thana Guzar-e-Faiz Bazar and the *havelis* of the Qazis. The other goes towards the *havelis* of Hakim Mohsin Khan, Muhammad 'Ali Khan, the *vakil* of the Rana; the house of Maulvi Rafi'-ud-Din Sahib[120] and of other people; and the *havelis* of Mir Najaf 'Ali Khan, the royal *faujdar*. Near this is Syed Amir 'Ali's house, the houses of Mirza Mughal, the *mukhtar* of Mirza Salim Bahadur Murshidzadah,[121] and the way to Faiz Bazar. The third street goes past the *haveli* of Mehdi Quli Khan Kasi who was a servant of Nawab Najaf Khan Bahadur. Near the *haveli* is an old mosque, called the Daiwali Masjid.

---

[114] Khwaja Mir 'Dard' was a noted Sufi and renowned poet; he died in 1785.

[115] A *hakim* as well as a poet who wrote under the pen-name 'Firaq', Sanaullah died some time before 1834.

[116] The Nawab of Jhajjar, a *jagir* that had been given by the East India Company to his father Nijabat 'Ali Khan. Both he and his father spent much of their time in Delhi.

[117] The first Nawab of Pataudi, whose small *jagir* was given in 1806 by the East India Company.

[118] A noble of the late eighteenth and early nineteenth centuries.

[119] Qassabpura literally means neighbourhood of butchers.

[120] Brother of Shah 'Abdul 'Aziz, 1749–1833.

[121] Son of Akbar II.

On the arch of the *dalan* of this mosque is the inscription:

[1] Thanks be to God that this mosque, through its glory, became a place of adoration to saintly persons.

[2] Wisdom announced the year of its foundation, 'Another Ka'ba has been populated'. [1064 /1653–54].[122]

Here there are the Chhatta La'l Miyan, where there are houses of the populace, the *haveli* of the late Hakim Faiz 'Ali Khan, the houses of Kashmiri Pandits, the *haveli* and Diwan Khana of Dayanandhan Pandit, *vakil* of the Raja of Ballabhgarh,[123] houses of other people, and the way to the city wall and the Dehli Gate.

Towards the northern steps of the Jama Masjid are some graves of elders, and shops of '*rang bhariye*' goldsmiths who make ornaments of enamel and plating. Besides this, there are shops of *paiwalas* and fireworks. From here a *kucha* goes towards Bazar Khanam, where there are shops of artisans, pedlars and the like, and some mosques. In this bazar is the *katra* of Kanwal Nain, known as 'Chakla'. This is the property of prostitutes. Blacksmiths and carpenters and others have their shops here. Here, above the gate of the garden of Munshi Sahib [Kanwal Nain], is inscribed the chronogram:

[1] This is such a place that the whole world beholds its beauty as it were a second heaven.

[2] It was built in the blink of an eye. Its year of making: the garden 'Kanwal Nain'. [1219/1804]

Its other gate is towards the elephant house of Mirza Wali Ahd Bahadur.[124] From this

---

[122] Zafar Hasan, Vol. I, p. 38.

[123] Ballabhgarh was one of the principalities under the control of the British Resident of Delhi, and therefore an agent or *vakil* was stationed there.

[124] The heir apparent of Akbar II, i.e. the later Bahadur Shah 'Zafar'.

gate towards the Faiz Bazar is the *dargah* of Hazrat Shah Kalimullah Jahanabadi.[125]

Onwards from this bazar are the shops of Lala Sant Lal, his *havelis* and the Rehet ka Kuan,[126] called '*charkhcheh*' in Persian. From here water goes to the tank in the Jama Masjid for *wuzu*'. Near this are Kucha-e-Ustad Hamid[127] and other *kuchas*. Towards the *haveli* of Sukh Lal Mahajan and the *dera* of Sukh Chand are several other *kuchas*. There is the Kucha Anar and other lanes, lanes from the *tiraha*, the *haveli* of the Nagar Seth and the way to the Bazar-e-Khanam. There are shops of artisans like gemstone-setters, goldsmiths and silversmiths, gilt-platers, and polishers. There is the Dariba Police Chowki. There is also the Bala Khana of Shaikh Badr-ud-Din 'Ali Khan, the seal-engraver, who is unparalleled in calligraphy and craftsmanship.[128] Near it is the shop of Kanjas *halwa'i*.[129] Next to this shop is a lane that leads to the *haveli* and *kothi* of Lala Mangat Rai and Sansari Mal. In its neighbourhood are also Chhatta Shahji, Roshanpura, Gali Masjid Khajoor Wali, the *havelis* of Lala Sukh Chand Mahajan, Lala Bakhshi Ram Gudwale, Jatti Balkishan, Lala Mohan Lal, Makhan Lal, and the houses of other common people.

In front of the above-mentioned *halwa'i*'s shop are the *madarsa* and mosque of Nawab Sharf-ud-Daulah Bahadur. On its central arch is the following chronogram:

[1] In the time of the king who has the sun for his throne and who is the shadow of God, the moon of the earth and the king of the age;

[2] Nasir-ud-Din who is [called] Muhammad Shah and whose sword annihilates the incredulity [*kufr*] of the age;

[3] Sharf-ud-Daulah has built a grand mosque and school.

[4] Wisdom said the chronogram of the date of its foundation '[It is] the *qibla* of the pilgrimage of the believers.'[130]

---

[125] Shaikh Kalimullah (1650–1729), grandson of Ustad Ahmad, the architect of the Red Fort, and the son of Nurullah, who was the calligrapher for the Jama Masjid. Shaikh Kalimullah took the Sufi path and revived the Chishti Sufi order in Delhi.

[126] A well fitted with a Persian wheel, a device to raise water.

[127] Ustad Hamid was one of the two chief architects of the Red Fort.

[128] Badr-ud-Din's skill was well-acknowledged. Even the seal of the Governor General of India was engraved by him.

[129] A street called Gali Kanjas now commemorates the *halwa'i*.

[130] Zafar Hasan, Vol. I, p. 138. The chronogram gives the date 1135, which corresponds to 1722–23. Sharf-ud-Daulah was a nobleman during the reign of Muhammad Shah.

Near this is the house of Hakim Mir 'Ali Sahib, son of Hakim Mir Hasan deceased, shops of *sarrafs* [bankers], *kothis* of *mahajans* [bankers] and Katra Mashru'.[131] Common people live here. The Khooni Darwaza of Dariba is also located here.

South of Sa'dullah Khan Chowk, towards Koh-e-Bari, are the shops of fowlers and butchers, and the royal elephant house. Close by is the Rajghat Police Chowki building, near which is located the Sunehri Masjid of Nawab Bahadur Khan Khwaja Sara.[132] In this mosque, in a cell to the south, the relics of Hazrat Sayyid-ush-Shuhada Imam Husain are kept. On the four sides of this cell, in golden letters, these words are written:

> O Allah, send blessings to Muhammad and his family, and bless and grant salvation to the rest of the others.

On the northern side of this cell, this is written:

> [1]   This holy hair which pleased to say the *durud* [a prayer]. The signs of victory were for the novice.
> [2]   We said that it belonged to his family. The angels said: 'the victorious lion of Allah'.

The Messenger of Allah said, may Allah's blessings be upon him and on his family and grant salvation to Anas. Blessings on those who visit my grave and it would be incumbent upon me to intercede for them on the Day of Judgement. [Anas narrates that when the Messenger of Allah cut off his hair] Abu Talha was the first one who took one of his hairs.

Inside the *mihrab*, at the head of the threshold of the cell, is written:

> I have put my trust in Allah.
> The hair of the pure *imam–king* of the martyrs, may peace be upon him, your intercession, O Messenger of Allah.

---

131 *Mashru'* is a special kind of fabric.

132 Nawab Bahadur Javed Khan was the chief eunuch of the harem during the reign of Muhammad Shah; during the reign of his successor, Ahmad Khan, he was the power behind the throne, together with Qudsia Begam, the mother of the young emperor.

[1] O Lord, by the receiving of the Messenger of humans and jinns. O Lord, by the mourners of Badr and Hunain

[2] My sins, make in two parts and pass one half to Hasan, and grant one half to Husain.

[3] O Haidar the Rider, it is the time of need! O fount of eight and four, it is the time of need.

[4] A difficult task has befallen me. O wielder of the Zulfiqar, it is the time of need.

On both sides of this building, above the doors, the first *kalima* and the Prophetic *hadith* are inscribed.

Behind this Sunehri Masjid is the tomb of the late Bhaggo Begam, the wife of Hazrat Firdaus Manzil [Shah 'Alam], which is famous as Koh-e-Bari. Here, on the western door of the above-mentioned mosque are written the words:

> The large western door of this blessed *khanqah* is where people pay respect to the Prophet, may peace be upon him.

After this the Akbarabadi mosque is located. On its entrance an inscription is written in the Naskh script:

> This mosque is intended for the use of men only and it is such a place where the heart is at peace. The *Hammam-e-Nizamat* and *Chauk-e-Dilkusha* are located here. These are buildings where all seekers of truth observe prayers; and for the non-believers this place refreshes the soul. For the departed, it is a place of recreation, and for those of the mortal world, it is a place of gain. This mosque was built in Shihab-ud-Din Muhammad Shah Jahan's reign, in the name of his Begam A'za-un-Nisa, who was also called Akbarabadi Begam. It was meant with the intent and hope for reward and salvation. All the expenses related to the mosque (both internal and external spending) were met through the *waqf* [trust]; so much so that when needed, its repairs could also be paid for through this trust. The rest of the money was put aside for the mosque, the *hammam* [tank], the students of the *madarsa*, and those who were in need, the poor (who have not been mentioned by name). These structures were built in two years, after an expense of 1.5 lakhs, and they were completed at the

end of the month of Ramzan, from the twenty-fifth regnal year of the King, i.e. 1006 *Hijri*. May God reward the King for this task. Amen.

It has seven doorways, of which the central one is larger than the others and over which the *surat Al-Fajr* is inscribed.[133]

Near this mosque are the Kashmiri Katra and the building of the mint. In this *katra* is the grave of Haji Haramain, houses of the common people, and the *haveli* of Khan-e-Dauran Khan. In the reign of Muhammad Shah, Khan-e-Dauran Khan was the lord of five lakh infantry and cavalry, and held the positions of the 'Amir-ul-Umara', 'Bakhshi-ul-Mulk'. In this lane are the houses of Nawab Faiz Muhammad Khan. Next to this is the gate of Daryaganj. There is another lane here where the *sarai* and houses of Miyan Sabir Bakhsh,[134] and the mosque of Nawab Raushan-ud-Daulah are located. On the arch of the *dalan* of the mosque is this inscription:

[1] Thanks be to God, that by the blessings of the grace of the Sayyid, a protection of the knowledge [of God], Shah Bhik, who is a perfect and holy teacher;

[2] In the reign of a king glorified like Alexander and dignified like Jamshed, the spreader of justice, Muhammad Shah, the champion of the faith, and king;

[3] Raushan-ud-Daulah Zafar Khan, the lord of beneficence and bounty, built this golden mosque resembling heaven.

[4] Such a mosque that its dignified open courtyard the sky sweeps every morning with the pencil of the sun's rays.

[5] Its clear tank represents the stream of Paradise; whoever performs ablutions with its water becomes pure of his sins.

[6] The date of its foundation Rasai obtained from the invisible inspiration: '[It is a] mosque like the mosque of Jerusalem where the light of God descends.'[135] [1157 / 1744–45]

---

[133] Note by Qasimi, p. 176. The mosque was built in 1650. The *surat Al-Fajr* is the eighty-ninth chapter of the Quran, called 'The Dawn'. This grand mosque was demolished in the aftermath of the revolt of 1857.

[134] Shah Sabir Bakhsh was a leading Chishti Sufi; he died in 1820.

[135] Zafar Hasan, Vol. I, p. 33. The date corresponds to 1714–15. 'Roshan-ud-Daulah' was the title of Khwaja Muzaffar, a prominent noble during the reigns of Farrukhsiyar and Muhammad Shah.

The interior of this mosque is decorated with gilt-work. Behind the mosque is the house of the *qazi*. From here onwards, one lane leads to the above-mentioned Tiraha Bairam Khan, the building of the Faiz Bazar Police Chowki, the *havelis* of Nawab Saifullah Khan,[136] Nawab Qamar-ud-Din Khan, Muhammad Amin Khan,[137] and the *haveli* and mosque of Hakim Bu 'Ali Khan. This mosque bears this chronogram on the front:

[1]   Bu 'Ali Khan had this mosque constructed on the orders of the ruler.

[2]   Angels, tell the year of its date [of construction]: 'This is the second Masjid-e-Aqsa.' [1226/1811]

Muhammad Khan Karora's *sarai* is also here.

Near the Dehli Gate of the city are the houses of Rai Pran Kishen, Lala Gor Parshad and others. Near the building of the Faiz Bazar Police Chowki is a lane which opens towards the garden of Nawab Bahadur 'Ali Khan and the gate of Daryaganj. Here are the *kothis* of British officials, cantonment of the city troops, the Tope Khana building, *kothis* of Lamter [?] merchant and Nawab Ahmad Bakhsh Khan Bahadur, and the Zinat-ul-Masajid mosque.[138]

A description of the Zinat-ul-Masjid mosque

Inside the mosque, towards the north, is a tomb. Its outer screen enclosure is made of red stone, and the inner enclosure, the floor and the gravestone of Zinat-un-Nisa Begam are made of marble. On the wall next to this grave, in the Sulus script, this *ayat* is engraved:

---

[136] A noble whose career spanned the reigns of several Mughal emperors, from Aurangzeb to Muhammad Shah.

[137] Prime minister of Muhammad Shah for a short period, 1720–21. He was the father of Nawab Qamar-ud-Din Khan and nephew of Nizam-ul-Mulk Asaf Jah, the founder of the state of Hyderabad.

[138] The mosque was built by Zinat-un-Nisa Begam, a daughter of Aurangzeb.

Say: 'O my Servants who have transgressed against their souls! Despair not of the Mercy of Allah: for Allah forgives all sins: for He is Oft-Forgiving, Most Merciful.' [39:53]

Our friend, he who comforts the heart, is buried here. It is God's grace that the grave is blessed.
Zinat-un-Nisa Begam, hopeful of blessings, the daughter of Badshah Muhiyuddin Muhammad 'Alamgir Ghazi [Aurangzeb]: 1122 *Hijri* [1710–11].

Near this is the gate of the city wall, the magazine and the house of Kunwar Raj Singh, Raja of Ballabhgarh. The policing of the neighbourhood of the *Dar-ul-Khilafa* is entrusted to this Raja. Here are the residential bungalows of the English Sahibs, the *kothi* of Nawab Faiz Muhammad Khan and the Neela Burj of the city wall. In the north of Sa'dullah Khan's *chowk*, towards the Lahori Gate of the Qil'a-e-Mubarak ['auspicious fort', i.e. Red Fort], on one side is the fort, and on the other side, the gate of Munshi Kanwal Nain's garden, the residences of people, the elephant house of the heir-apparent and the Urdu Bazar. This bazar is right in front of the gate of the Qil'a-e-Mubarak.

From the Lahori Gate of the Qil'a-e-Mubarak to the Lahori Gate of the city
Towards the northern bazar, first come the *kothis* of Dibbey Sahib and Cutton [?] Sahib, and the Qazi ki Masjid. On this mosque, this inscription is engraved:

[1]   Praise be to God! We sing the praise of the Prophet.
[2]   May our wishes be heard and granted.
[3]   This mosque was built during 'Alamgir's reign,
[4]   By the light of God, to gain happiness.
[5]   We hope that here his worship continues. [1090 /1679–80]

Inside the mosque, at the place where the *imam* stands, above the *mihrab*, this *ayat* is engraved in the Sulus script:

O ye who believe! Bow down, prostrate yourselves, and adore your Lord; and do good; that ye may prosper. [22:77]

Near the mosque are the shops of Manuel Sahib,[139] the *haveli* of Daulat-un-Nisa Begam, the house of Bhag Singh, the *kothi* of Zeb-un-Nisa[140] Begam Sahiba, wife of Samru Sahib, and the shops of *kaghazis*. These shops belong to Sukh Chand Sahu.

The *Tirpolia*

Here is the house of Sukh Chand *mahajan*, the *mandi* of flower-sellers, Sharab Khana [a place selling alcohol], Mumtaz Ganj and the royal arsenal. After this is the Kaudia Pul under which the Faiz Nahar flows. After this is a junction of three streets, from which one street goes towards the *mahal* of Nawab Sahiba. Another goes towards the house of 'Abdullah Khan. 'Abdullah Khan was a *mansabdar* in the time of Emperor Shah 'Alam. The third street goes towards the residences of the *kaghazis*, the common people and other houses. From the above-mentioned *tirpolia* emerges the way towards Kinari Bazar, Johari Bazar, *havelis*, the garden of Kham Begam and the mosque of Sa'id-ud-Daulah. The gate of this mosque has this inscription:

[1]   In the name of Allah, Most Gracious, Most Merciful. Allah is the Light of the heavens and the earth.

[2]   By the holy blessing and the favour of Ahmad [the Prophet] the foundation [of this building], which shows the *qibla* to the whole world, was laid.

[3]   In the auspicious reign of Ahmad Shah, the champion of the faith, the efforts of Sa'id-ud-Daulah were brought to perfection.

[4]   The invisible angel justly said, 'A duplicate of the exalted Ka'ba is constructed'. [1165– 66/1752–53]

Near this is Kucha-e-Natwan, where the common people live. Here are also the Imambarah of Mir 'Askari and Chandni Chowk, down the middle of which the Faiz Nahar flows. Here is also the gate of the Bagh-e-Sahibabad. This *bagh* is known as

---

[139]   Probably Manuel Deremao, who was a military freelancer, receiving a pension from the British as he had left Maratha service during the British conflict with the Marathas.

[140]   Begam Samru, a woman of humble origins who inherited the forces and estates of her husband who was a military adventurer, and became a politically powerful *zamindar* of the Delhi territory in the first decades of the nineteenth century. She built a grand, European-style building in Delhi which later came to be known as Bhagirath Palace.

Bagh-e-Begam. This had been founded by Jahan Ara, the daughter of Emperor Shah Jahan. Inside the garden are a *sarai*, an assembly hall and Khawaspura. The Faiz Nahar also flows through it. Here are also Kucha Qabil Attar, Katra Neel which has the houses of Khatris and the residence of Har Narayan Fotedar. In the same locality are Kucha Brij Nath, Kucha Ghasi Ram, Haveli Bakhshi Bhawani Shankar[141] and Chhatta Jan Nisar Khan. Jan Nisar Khan was a *mansabdar* of the time of Emperors Farrukhsiyar and Muhammad Shah who reached a high station. He was deceived by Burhan-ul-Mulk Sa'adat Khan and killed by Ajaju Zamindar,[142] who was at this time bent on rebellion and war against Burhan-ul-Mulk. Jan Nisar Khan's grave is in the *dargah* of Khwaja Baqi Billah. After this *kucha* is a lane by the name of Gandhi Gali, and Bazar-e-Mazid Parcha which has shops of cloth merchants and the *haveli* of Muhammad Bakhsh alias Mammu. Outside the Bazar-e-Mazid Parcha is the Katra Maidagaran,[143] on whose gate is inscribed:

In all alertness and in my senses, I thus claim that this sinner, I, Muhammad Bakhsh, have built these buildings with my own money: the *khanqah*, the mosque, all these holy places, located in Chidimar Tola, Kucha-e-Maidagaran, where *milad* is held in praise of the Prophet and where religious classes are conducted. This palace, where *tabarruk* is distributed, is a place with orchards, for which there will be holy reward [*sawab*]. I have built it myself and protected this auspicious building with respect due to it. It includes within it a *katra*, *manzil*, *haveli* and a garden as well. I have also fixed an amount in *waqf* for its upkeep, since this is the Prophet's guest house [*mehman khana*].

Upon entering the city near Lahori Gate, a piece of land has been exclusively put aside [as *waqf*] for the upkeep, so that whatever it yields, one-eleventh of it will be for restoring and looking after the buildings. The rest of the sum will be divided in two: one for the *milad* ceremonies and the other for all the other expenditure. The last half is for the person responsible for the keys and the caretaker. I myself

---

[141] Bhawani Shankar was the paymaster of Maratha troops. He switched to the British side when he saw that they were likely to be victorious, and he was suitably rewarded with estates by the British.

[142] Jan Nisar Khan was killed in 1731.

[143] Literally, flour-makers.

will pay for all other requirements. The *mutawallis* who come later are free to spend, but only according to the rules that have already been set. The keys of this legacy will be held by Muhammad Isma'il (the father of Ibrahim). All the buildings are to be used for sacred purposes. The *mutawalli* has accepted the responsibility given to him, and no one is allowed, till the Day of Reckoning, to interfere in this arrangement. I hope that they will come to the aid of the believers and if dishonest, then he will not receive God's and the Prophet's mercy.

This has been inscribed by Muhammad Rafi'.

Inside this *katra* live the populace, and outside are shopkeepers and the Kucha-e-Habsh Khan. Habsh Khan was one of the slaves of Aurangzeb. When he was about 115 years old he could still eat a whole roast sheep. He was very strong. In this lane is the property of Nawab Sa'adat Khan, the uncle of Nawab Safdar Jang, the *wazir* of Ahmad Shah.[144] Behind the *haveli* of the said *wazir* of Ahmad Shah is the mosque of Bu Sa'id Khan. On the arch of the *dalan* of this mosque is the inscription:

[1] In the reign of the monarch who is a protection to the world, a dispenser of justice and the king of the religion, Muhammad Shah the champion of the faith and having pomp like Jamshid;

[2] The chief of inquisitorial justice, who adorns the seat of Muhammadan law, raises the standards of religion and demolishes temples and idols.

[3] Built in Delhi a mosque grand like heaven, the beholding of which affords to sight the pleasure of seing the Ka'ba.

[4] Its courtyard is as spacious as the prospect of saintly persons and its dome is all painted like the dome of heaven.

[5] For the date of its completion the invisible angel said, 'A second Ka'ba erected by Bu Sa'id the generous.'[145]

---

[144] Sa'adat Khan was a merchant from Khurasan who came to India and rose rapidly in the Mughal service. He was appointed governor of Awadh in 1724. He died in 1739 in Delhi when Nadir Shah attacked and occupied the city. His son-in-law Safdar Jang received governorship after him, and in addition, prime ministership of the empire between 1748 and 1752. They laid the foundations of the independent state of Awadh.

[145] Zafar Hasan, Vol. I, pp. 171–72. Abu Syed was the hereditary *muhtasib* (inquisitor) of Delhi. The chronogram gives the date 1136, which corresponds to 1723–24. The mosque is known as Muhtasib's mosque.

In this lane is the *haveli* of Nawab 'Abbas Quli Khan, which is the property of the said Nawab Wazir. Here is the Katra Roghan Zard (i.e. Ghee ka Katra) and Nahar-e-Sa'adat Khan. Beside the said Nahar is the mosque of Nawab Ghazi-ud-Din Khan on which is inscribed:

[1] By the grace of God, Mustafa [the Prophet] and the king, Ghaziuddin Khan Bahadur, the follower of the strong religion;

[2] Brought into being a mosque on the canal for the people, every pillar of which is as strong as Alexander's wall.

[3] The water of the canal, on account of cleaning the wind of its court of the dust, became soul nourisher on the earth, like the water of Khizr (i.e. the fountain of life).

[4] Each of its eaves is attractive like the eye of the intoxicated beauties, every pillar and pier is firm like the wall of Alexander. [

5] Surely and certainly, his prayer is accepted, who rubs his forehead with its floor, niche and *mihrab*.

[6] The date of its foundation was said in poetry by the favour of God, 'The mosque of Ahmad was founded through compassion for worlds.'[146]

Near this are the Katra Gadibanan and the English-style house of Lala Har Narayan. Here are also Katra Sa'adat Khan, the house of Nawab Ahmad 'Ali Khan,[147] the *haveli* of Khan-e-Jahan and the Kabuli Gate of the city.

After the Kucha-e-Habsh Khan is Kucha-e-Chela, i.e. the *kucha* of Fateh Muhammad, a *chela* of Emperor Shah Jahan. Inside this are the *havelis* of the populace and of Nawab Shams-ud-Daulah, the *munshi* of Mirza Mahmud Khan Bahadur, other houses of the people and the Lahori Gate of the city.

---

146 Zafar Hasan, Vol. I, p. 176. Ghazi-ud-Din was the title of Ahmad Beg, who was an important nobleman in the first half of the eighteenth century. The chronogram gives the date 1140, which corresponds to 1727–28.

147 The Nawab of Rampur from 1790 to 1840. The Rampur Nawabs had connections in Delhi.

Description of the bazars on the south, proceeding from the Lahori Gate of the Qil'a-e-Mubarak to the Lahori Gate of the city

Here there are the Urdu Bazar, Bagh Kalali, the elephant house of Prince Mirza Jahangir and Kucha-e-Bulaqi Begam. The other way from here leads towards Dariba Kalan. There is the *haveli* of Puran tailor and a *kucha* which has houses of the common people. In this same locality are the post office and the Khooni Darwaza. In Dariba Kalan are the Katra Mashru', and the *havelis* and *kothis* of *mahajans*. On either side in this bazar are the shops of *sarrafs*, and the mosque of Sharf-ud-Daulah and the building of his *madarsa*. At the front of the hall of the mosque this chronogram is engraved:

Nasir-ud-Din Muhammad Shah, he is a king like the sun, like the moon of this world, whose sword destroys blasphemy. It is he who ordered Sharf-ud-Daulah to

build this magnificent mosque. There has thus been the coming together of two auspicious stars. The date of its building was arrived at thus: this is the *qiblah* of the believers. [1137/1724]

In front of this is the house of Hakim Mir 'Ali Sahib, son of the late Hakim Mir Hasan Sahib, and the shop of Kanjas *halwa'i*. Here all manner of sweets are prepared and are famous throughout the city. In front of this is a lane that leads to Dariba-e-Khurd,[148] Raushanpura, Chhatta-e-Shahji, Kucha-e-Ballimaran and Kucha-e-Jogiwadan. Common people live in Kucha-e-Jogiwadan. On one street from Kanjas *halwa'i*'s shop is the Dariba Police Chowki, the *haveli* of Nagar Seth, Kucha-e-Anar and other buildings; and towards the Jama Masjid is the Rehet ka Mohalla. At the Khooni Darwaza there are pedlar's shops and the Kotwali Chabutra[149] where prisoners are confined. In the bazar in front of the *chabutra* a stout stick is planted which is famous by the name of Lal Khan ka Lakkad. Criminals are tied to this and beaten. From very long ago a

---

[148] Dariba-e-Khurd now goes by the name of Kinari Bazar.

[149] Today this site is occupied by buildings of the Sisganj Gurudwara.

wheel was set up at this place and murderers were killed here. Adjoining the Kotwali Chabutra is the *madarsa* of Nawab Raushan-ud-Daulah. On the door of this *madarsa* these words in the Nasta'liq script are engraved on marble:

> This property has been kept in the *waqf* and Raushan-ud-Daulah Zafar Khan Bahadur had this *madarsa* built.

Within this, right next to the building of the *madarsa*, there is a mosque which was built by the same Nawab. On the central arch is inscribed:

[1] In the reign of the king of seven climes, Muhammad Shah, the sovereign who has Solomon-like splendour;

[2] This mosque was made unrivalled in the world for its magnificence, for Shah Bhik the pole star of the age.

[3] O God! It is not but for the sake of laying him under an obligation that it [the mosque] is named after Raushan-ud-Daulah Zafar Khan.

[4] Its date, calculated from the flight [of the Prophet] is one thousand one hundred and thirty four.[150]

In this area are the *havelis* of the people, the houses of Radha Kishan *vakil*, the shops of shoe-sellers, the house of Mirza Ashraf Beg,[151] his Sheesh Mahal, and the gate of the *kucha* of Dariba-e-Khurd. In this *kucha* are houses of *halwa'is*, Kunja Mal, *sarrafs*, cloth merchants and *joharis*. Here also live the *tawaifs* Lachhmi and Bi Jan. There is the *haveli* of Hakim Rukn-ud-Din Khan[152] and the gate of Kucha Maliwada. In this *gali* are the houses of Hakim Ajit Singh and other people, and the *haveli* of Captain Manuel and others.

After the gate of Dariba-e-Khurd are shops of gold lace-makers, sellers of gold and silver brocade and spangles, the entrance to the *haveli* of Rukn-ud-Din Khan,

---

[150] Zafar Hasan, Vol. I, p. 121. The date 1134 corresponds to 1721–22. For Raushan-ud-Daulah, see above.

[151] Mirza Ashraf Beg commanded the troops of Akbar II from 1809 till his death in 1831, and also enjoyed the confidence of the British.

[152] *Hakim* and poet, who received a title from the Mughal emperor.

the *kothi* of Lala Saudagar Mal, the *haveli* of Ibrahim 'Ali Khan and Najaf 'Ali Khan, the sons of Lutf 'Ali Khan, the Bazzazon ka Katra,[153] Katra Ashrafi, Katra Nandu, and Kucha Khan Chand. Inside is the *haveli* of the prince of Balkh, 'Abdur Rahman Khan, a son of Nazr Muhammad Khan. When Emperor Shah Jahan conquered Balkh, he imprisoned its people, i.e. its princes, and brought them here. After a while the emperor exalted these prisoners with royal favours and gave them permission to return to Balkh. One of these princes, who has been mentioned above, stayed back in the service of the emperor and made his house in this *muhalla*.

After this come Chandni Chowk, and the garden and *hammam* of Jahan Ara Begam. In this *chowk* are the shops of saddle-makers and other artisans. After this are the Kucha-e-Rai Man[154] and the *haveli* of Ghulam Murtaza Khan,[155] the brother of Mansur, and others. Besides this, there is the *haveli* of Mir 'Azimullah and Mir Khurd. From this *kucha* lies the way to Colonel Skinner's *haveli*. Near this *kucha* are shops of grocers and *attars* [druggists, perfumers]. Here is the Naichabandon ka Kucha[156] where there are houses of the people and shops of *huqqa*-tube binders and raw silk-sellers. Here is located the house of 'Inayatullah Khan, the *haveli* of Hakim Ghulam 'Ali Khan, the house

---

[153] This means the *katra* of cloth merchants.

[154] Named after Yehia Rai Man, killed during the occupation of the city by Nadir Shah, in 1739. The street is now more popularly, but incorrectly, called Kucha Rehman.

[155] Ghulam Murtaza Khan was a well-known painter, active from 1809 to 1830.

[156] Literally, 'the street of the *huqqa*-tube binders', i.e. manufacturers of *huqqa* tubes.

of Nawab Najaf Quli Khan,[157] the residence of Nawab Hisam-ud-Din Haidar Khan, the *haveli* of Hakim Miyan Jan, the house of 'Azimullah Khan alias Mir Khairati. One *kucha* leads to the *havelis* of Nawab Faizullah Beg Khan and of the late Hakim Sharif Khan[158] and the mosque built by him. On the central arch of this mosque is inscribed:

[1] Thanks be to God that by the efforts of Muhammad Sharif Khan a mosque is erected which is the Ka'ba of purity.

[2] When the Muazzin's call arose, the preacher of wisdom said, 'Seek the year of its foundation from the house of God'.[159]

Then there is the *haveli* belonging to Nawab Ahmad Bakhsh Khan, which was built by Skinner Sahib Bahadur.[160] On its gate is written: 'Haveli-e-Kaptan James Skinner Sahib Bahadur – 1811 *Isvi*'.

In front of this is the Kucha-e-Jogiwada, the *havelis* of Imam Quli Beg Khan, the house of Mirza Qalandar Beg Khan, the *darogha* of the royal *Kaili Khana*, the *haveli* of Sher Afgan Khan who was a big *amir* in the time of 'Alamgir Aurangzeb. Here there is the house of Munshi Barkat 'Ali Khan, which was built by Maulvi Fazl-e-Imam Sahib.[161] From here one lane goes towards Maliwada.

After this is the *haveli* of Bakhshi Bhawani Shankar, the shops of *charkhewalas*,[162] the house of Munshi Tek Chand, Kucha Peepal Mahadev, the *havelis* of Sufiullah Yar

---

[157] He was a protégé of Najaf Khan, the energetic minister and general of the reign of Shah 'Alam II.

[158] Hakim Sharif Khan (1725–1807) was a renowned *hakim* and the founder of a line of eminent *hakims*. He was also a teacher and author of important treatises, who pioneered a closer connection between Ayurvedic and Unani traditions of medicine.

[159] Zafar Hasan, Vol. I, p. 105. The chronogram is somewhat uncertain. Zafar Hasan works it out as giving the date 1261 *Hijri*, which corresponds to 1781–82. Qasimi also points to the possibility of it being 1196 *Hijri*. See Qasimi, p. 186.

[160] James Skinner, of mixed British and Indian parentage, was one of a number of military freelancers who flourished in north India in the second half of the* eighteenth century. He initially made his home in Delhi in Ballimaran, but soon after sold it to make a mansion near Kashmiri Gate.

[161] Fazl-e-Imam Khairabadi was a learned scholar who held a judicial post under the British in the early nineteenth century.

[162] According to one conjecture, this refers to the manufacturers of *charkhis*, or wheel-shaped firecrackers. Chenoy, *Shahjahanabad*, p. 57.

Khan and Raja Jai Sukh Rai and others,[163] the house of the sons of Hakim Baqa, and the houses of common people. Next to the shops of the *charkhewalas* is the *haveli* of Haingan *tawaif*. From here one street leads to Raushanpura. In this direction lies the *haveli* of Lala Mohan Lal, the houses of other people, the *chhatta* of Lala Tan Sukh Rai, the *kothi* of Lala Sukh Chand, the houses of Bakhshi Ram Gudwale, Mohalla Masjid Khajur, and the *kucha* and *dera* constructed by Lala Sukh Chand. From here one way leads to Kucha-e-Anar and the *havelis* of the populace, the *kothi* of Lala Fayii Chand, and the houses of Lala Sukh Lal and others.

From the Kucha Ballimaran

Here is the Chandni Chowk Police Chowki, which is connected to the Kotwali Chabutra. Near this is the Rewdiwalon ka Katra and the *haveli* of Nawab Hyder Quli[164] which is the *riyasat* of coachmen. Here is the Masjid Fatehpuri Begam, which was constructed by Fatehpuri Begam, a wife of Emperor Shah Jahan. To the south of the mosque is a bazar where there are the Katra Ghulam Muhammad Khan, Katra Gondi and other buildings, the shop of Hafiz Ilahi Bakhsh the pedlar, and the shops of the Fatehpuri Masjid. Behind the mosque is a *katra* built by Fatehpuri Begam, which has shops of the *maidagars*, Kucha-e-Khari Baoli, shops of grocers and *batashawalas*, and shops of Muhammad Amin the *attar*. Also in this area are Kucha-e-Naya Bans, and the Chowki and *thana* building of the Lahori Gate Police, which is right next to the Lahori Gate.

From the Lahori Gate of the Qil'a-e-Mubarak to the Fatehpuri Masjid the Faiz Nahar flows through the middle of the bazar: 'This is the interesting market of the *chowk*. One stops wherever the heart is captivated'.

From the Lahori Gate of the Qil'a-e-Mubarak

Here lies the *chhatta* of Nigambodh Ghat. Within this are houses of the rich and Hindu temples. Here is the territory of oarsmen and the Police Chowki. On the bank of the Jamuna there are *ghats*, *chhatris* and Hindu temples. Further on is the Nigambodh Gate, the city wall, the houses of *bans* and *balliwalas*, the graveyard of the English Sahibs,[165]

---

[163] A banker who was in charge of the royal finances during the early part of the reign of Akbar II and enjoyed the confidence of Mumtaz Mahal, the royal consort.

[164] A nobleman of the reign of Muhammad Shah.

[165] i.e. the Lothian Cemetery.

the *haveli* of Dara Shukoh,[166] titled 'Shah Bilawal Khan', the
son of Shah Jahan Badshah-e-Ghazi, Sahib Qiran-e-Sani. Near
the door of the *haveli* of this prince is a cannon. This is fired
twice in the day, early in the morning and at night. Near this is
the *sarjan* [sergeant's] bungalow, the barrack, i.e. the camp of
the artillery, and the magazine. To the left of the camp are the
special lines of the cavalry. There is also the *haveli* of the late
Nawab Safdar Jang Mansur 'Ali Khan. Behind it are the houses
of the *kaghazis*, the grave of Shah Abadani Sahib, the gate

of the garden of Begam Samru and the enclosure of the soldiers of her camp, and a
settlement of grass-cutters. Behind the *haveli* of Nawab Safdar Jang is a *hammam* and
the Faiz Nahar flows there. Towards the Qil'a-e-Mubarak, behind the garden of Begam
Samru and towards the west, is the house of Akhterloni [Ochterlony][167] Sahib and the
kothi of Katan [Cutton?] Sahib. After the houses of these gentlemen is the *kothi* of the
Resident of the *Dar-ul-Khilafa* Shahjahanabad, Kela Ghat, the gate of the city wall, and
the bank of the river. Here there are the *haveli* of Nawab 'Abdullah Khan and a mosque.[168]
In the southern part of this mosque, in its outer hall, these words are engraved:

> This mosque was built in 1154 *Hijri*, during the reign of Muhammad Shah Badshah,
> by 'Abdul Majeed Khan Mujib-ud-Daulah and through his property in *waqf* he
> undertook the repair of the bazar as well as the upkeep of the mosque.

Here is the Katra-e-Badalpura, the *kothi* of Dundee Sahib, the building of the
English post office, the camp of the battalion of Dundee Sahib, the way that leads
in the direction of Nasir Ganj,[169] the way to the *haveli* of Sahiba Mahal, the stable of
Dara Shukoh, and houses of the common people. There is the Zinat Badi and a garden
which contains the graves of princes and Zinat-un-Nisa Begam. The gravestone bears

---

166 This building is today known as Dara Shukoh's library.

167 Major General David Ochterlony was the first British Resident after the British took over the city in
     1803.

168 'Abdul Majeed Khan was a nobleman of the mid-eighteenth century.

169 Nasir Ganj was a market set up for profit by Ochterlony, and named after his Mughal title, Nasir-ud-
     Daulah. In the 1830s, James Skinner purchased this land to build St James's Church.

the *ayat Al-Kursi*[170] in Tughra form and the date 1116 (1704–05). On the headstone of a grave is written 'Tajdar Begam'. Also here is the grave of Muhammad Mahfuz, son of Khwaja Mu'in-ud-Din, where these verses are written:

> [1] Many months will come before we pass from this world, when flowers will bloom in the spring.
>
> [2] After which a day will come when we will become one with the dust. [949/1561]

Near this is the Katra-e-Mewa, which is also called Katra-e-Punjabi. Here is the Police Chowki of I'tiqad Khan, the *bangla* of Sayyid Firoz, the handprint of Hazrat Shah Mardan, may the blessings of Allah be upon him, and the famous Gali Kanchani. There is a street towards the Mori Gate of the city. From I'tiqad Khan's Police Chowki lie the *mohalla* Dhobiwada, Peepalwala Kuan, the house of Ismai'l Khan Risaldar in the special lines, and a lane towards the Kabuli Gate of the city wall. In this area are the *haveli* of Ismai'l Khan, the house of Syed Razi Khan,[171] the residences of the common people, and the Kabuli Gate of the city, from where the Faiz Nahar enters the city.

From behind the *kothi* of the Resident Bahadur of Dehli, one street leads to the Kashmiri Gate. In the midst of this bazar is the Police Chowki of Kashmiri Gate. After this is the *kothi* of Colonel James Skinner Sahib, near which is a mosque. On its door is written its name, 'Fakhr-ul-Masajid'. Over the arch this verse is inscribed:

> [1] The Khan, the cherisher of religion, Shuja'at Khan got a place in Paradise, by the will of God and for the sake of Murtaza ['Ali].
>
> [2] The chief of ladies, Kaniz Fatima, the pride of the world, built this mosque in his memory by the grace of Mustafa [the Prophet].[172]

Inside the mosque is written:

---

170 The *ayat Al-Kursi*: Quran, 2:255.

171 Syed Razi Khan was a respected person who was used as a channel of everyday communication between Akbar II and the British Resident.

172 Zafar Hasan, Vol. I, p. 183. Zafar Hasan has added the date '1141 Hijri' (1728–29) under the inscription. Shujat Khan was a nobleman at Aurangzeb's court; he died in 1672–73.

There is no God but Allah, and Muhammad is His Messenger.

Facing this mosque is Nasir Ganj. Here there is a path to Kashmiri Gate and the camp of the Telinga battalion.[173]

Description of the environs of *Dar-ul-Khilafa* Shahjahanabad

From Mahabat Khan ki Reti, where his *haveli* is situated,[174] towards the Neel Burj of the *Dar-ul-Khilafa* – here in the sands there is a famous *takiya* [hospice] of a *faqir*, which is known as '*Nakte ka takiya*'. In front of the Rajghat Gate is the *takiya* of Shah Bade Sahib, and Salimgarh. This is also called Nurgarh. It was constructed by Salim Shah, son of Sher Shah. Close to this is a dome which is called the Neeli Chhatri. Emperor Humayun had this constructed in 939 [1532–33]. He often sat there and viewed the river. Many people call this the *bangla* of Jahangir Shah, and Hindu gentlemen say that this *chhatri* has been present here from ancient times and that Emperor Jahangir had it constructed afresh, demolishing the vestiges of it and remaking it in the form of a *bangla*. But this claim of the Hindus is without foundation because there is a couplet inscribed on the building, which was composed by Emperor Jehangir himself, that attests to the construction of it by Emperor Humayun. In Taimur's lineage, Humayun is given the title 'Jannat Ashiyani' after his death. On an arch within the building is written:

> Allah is great
>
> By Emperor Jahangir, son of Emperor Akbar
>
> What a graceful and happy place, the seat of 'Jannat Ashyani'.[175]

At present the *chhatri* is occupied by 'Ali Shah Darvesh Banwa.[176]

From here towards the north, near the city wall, is the Qudsia Bagh, which the

---

[173] The word is used for infantry soldiers.

[174] Mahabat Khan was commander-in-chief and governor of Delhi during the reign of Shah Jahan. The site where his *haveli* stood is now occupied by the Income Tax Office (ITO) complex.

[175] Zafar Hasan, Vol. II, p. 299. Zafar Hasan cites a longer inscription and adds a date, 1028 *Hijri* [1618–19].

[176] Since then the building has been converted into a temple.

common people call 'Kursia Bagh'. This garden was laid by Nawab Qudsia Begam.[177] This is at the moment controlled by Mirza Abu Zafar Bahadur,[178] the heir-apparent. Adjacent to the city wall at Kashmiri Gate is the *kothi* of Dr Ludlow Sahib.[179] After this is the *bagh* and *kothi* of Dundee Sahib. Near the Kabuli Gate of the city, on a hill, is the grave of Pir-e-Ghaib.[180] Near it, on the hill itself, is the *kothi* of Fraser Sahib, which was built in 1235 [1819–20]:

[1] Should anyone pass by this way,
    They would see a pleasant *kothi*.

[2] They would see a tall white building,
    Which has twice the radiance of the moon.

[3] The moonlight scattered all around,
    The advent of the winter, the cool breeze,

[4] The appearance of the white moon in the sky,
    A time of radiance from evening to morning.[181]

Here there was a pillar of hard stone, which had been brought by Emperor Firoz Shah. But now this pillar is broken in many places and has fallen from its place. On its broken pieces letters are inscribed in the following manner. Since this kind of pillar is also standing in Firoz Shah's Kotla, it will be mentioned in the section on the Kotla. The letters are these:

く， 869336

Next to the Kabuli Gate, on the public road towards the north, is the *takiya* of Bholu

177 Qudsia Begam, the wife of Muhammad Shah, was the mother of his son and successor Ahmad Shah, and with Javed Khan the eunuch, the poser behind the latter's throne. See note 135 on Javed Khan.

178 He ascended the throne in 1837 as Bahadur Shah II.

179 Dr Ludlow was the civil surgeon and was also consulted by the Mughal royal family. He built a grand mansion, which people facetiously referred to as 'Ludlow Castle'.

180 The building, which was a hunting lodge built by Firoz Shah Tughlaq in the mid-fourteenth century, was later named after a saint called Pir Ghaib, who lived here.

181 These are lines of poetry in Urdu that are in Sangin Beg's text. It is not implied, however, that they were to be found on the building itself.

Shah Faqir. After this is the tomb of Zeb-un-Nisa Begam and a red-stone mosque.[182] There are two chambers here. In Zeb-un-Nisa's chamber, the headstone of the grave carries an inscription [in Arabic] in the Sulus script:

> In the name of Allah, Most Gracious, Most Merciful.
> All that is on earth will perish. This is the grave of the great house of the culpable sinner, may she be welcomed in the mercy of the Honoured, Most Compassionate, Most Merciful, the *hafiza* Zeb-un-Nisa, who longed to be among the servants of the Lord of the worlds, [those] who are called to [His] forgiveness and good pleasure. The date of her death: May I be allowed into my heaven. [1113/1701–02]

On the headstone of the grave of the wife of Emperor Muhammad Shah, these words are inscribed:

[1] Muhammad Shah, who is the pride of kings, his wife: the daughter of Farrukhsiyar, who was himself the envoy of kings in his time.

[2] She was the sun in the sky of the sultanate and was the apple of his eye; she has passed away from this world.

[3] And on the Day of Judgement, may she be with Hazrat Fatima and may her soul be with the pure who have passed on.

[4] Her name was Malika-e-Zamani, her mother was Sayyida and her supporter was Hazrat 'Ali's Prophet.

[5] May she benefit from the holiness of the Prophet, as she revered the Prophet and all those who pledged their allegiance to him. [1203 /1789]

At the bottom of the tombstone this is inscribed:

> The iilumined grave of the honourable late Malika-e-Zamani: 1203 *Hijri*.

---

[182] Zeb-un-Nisa was the daughter of Aurangzeb. She was an accomplished Persian poet, a skilled calligrapher and the author of a commentary on the Quran. Her tomb was demolished when the railway line was laid in the second half of the nineteenth century.

From the Kabuli Gate to Shalimar, there is a highway. On this, first on the left hand, is the enclosure of Mirza Amir Beg Khan, son of Jamal Beg Khan 'Arab. Then there is the settlement called Mughal Pura, followed by the Sabzi Mandi where all sorts of seasonal vegetables and fruits, such as mangoes, *ber*, pomegranates, are sold. In the vicinity of the Sabzi Mandi are gardens. These gardens are known by the names of Raushan Ara, Bagh-e-Sirhindi, Bagh-e-Fiday Khan, Bagh-e-Qara Khan and Bagh-e-Chakbikram. Here there are streams; on the right hand is the Faiz Nahar which flows towards the city. Near the Sabzi Mandi is an enclosure which is known by the name of Bagh-e-Darbar Khan. On the gate of this enclosure, the following words are inscribed:

> These buildings, *sarais*, the mosque, *khanqah* and shops were built by Darbar Khan. He has made a *waqf* for these. The land towards the north and east is to support the building and maintenance of these properties. The date of its construction is 1076 [1665–66].

After this is the mosque and garden of Jawahar Khan. At the top of the entrance of this mosque these words are inscribed:

During the reign of 'Alamgir-e-'Adil, whose successful rule made this land a paradise, Jawahar Khan built the mosque and garden for his salvation. The prophetic voice said: 'May his garden bloom and this mosque thrive, as it is the axis [qibla] of this world.' [1066/1655–56]

Ahead of this are a *tirpolia* and the garden of Mahaldar Khan, the *nazir* of Emperor Muhammad Shah. On either side of the *tirpolia* this chronogram is inscribed:

[1] By the grace of God and the Prophet of the age [Muhammad], Mahaldar Khan Nazir built,

[2] Such a road, bazar and *tirpolia* that the event may be marked in the revolutions of the world.

[3] There came a voice from the invisible crier, 'May this house be everlasting.'[183]

The Bagh-e-Nazir has the following inscription:

[1] God has fulfilled hundreds of desires in this world, and this house was built by the grace of the true God.

[2] For the chronogram of the garden I said clearly, 'The devoted (slave) Muhammad Mahaldar Khan.'

[3] Ghulam-e-Nabi [slave of the Prophet] Nazir Mahaldar Khan dedicated the garden of Paradise to God.[184]

After this is the garden of Patni Mal, the garden of Kakwan and Mubarak Bagh, which has been recently laid out by the Resident of the *Dar-ul-Khilafa*, Jarnail Sahib (General Ochterlony). Near the *mauza-e-Sahipur* is the *kothi* of Nawab Ahmad Bakhsh Khan. Here there is a fork in the road. One road leads towards Shalimar Bagh where there is another fork. In the Shalimar Bagh[185] is the *kothi* of the Resident Sahib. This garden and its *kothis* have been constructed by Charles Theophilus Metcalfe Sahib. Here there

---

[183] Zafar Hasan, Vol. II, p. 271. The date derived from the chronogram is 1141 *Hijri*, i.e. 1728–29.

[184] Zafar Hasan, Vol. II, p. 270. The date of the chronogram is 1122 *Hijri*, i.e. 1710–11.

[185] Shalimar Bagh was a royal garden laid out in the time of Shah Jahan. Aurangzeb was crowned here in 1658.

is an army camp, special lines and such, and a few houses which have recently been constructed by Jarnail Sahib. On the second fork from the above-mentioned *mauza* is the Sarai Badli, where there is the Police Sarkar. From here to *mauza-e-Narela* are a few rural settlements. After that is the town of Sonipat. This is an old *qasba*. Below the fort next to the settlement of the city is the *dargah* of Imam Nasir-ud-Din. Imam Nasir-ud-Din and Mir Ibrahim are buried in the same grave. Mir Ibrahim was the nephew of Imam Nasir-ud-Din. Both were martyred on the same day in battle with the unbelievers.[186] According to the chronograms, the life and date of death of these two elders are concealed, after subtracting the word 'budand' [was], in the following verse:

Abu Muhammad was the *imam* of the age.[187]

This quatrain is engraved in the Nasta'liq script on the eastern side of the dome:

Mir Ibrahim and Nasir-ud-Din of the age
Light of the two worlds, two eyes of the body of uprightness
[It is] the good fortune of Sonipat that
Two honoured ones are buried here.

Close to the *dargah* is a mosque. This mosque was repaired during the reign of Shah Ghiyas-ud-Din Ghori, whose grave is located in Khwaja Qutb-ud-Din.[188] Inside this mosque, this is written [from the Quran]:

There is no God but He ... (till the *ayat*) ... He is Most Compassionate, Most Merciful.

---

186 This is believed to be the oldest *dargah* in India. The account recorded in later Gazetteers is somewhat different from the conventional explanation of 'martyred by unbelievers' given by Sangin Beg. Imam Nasir-ud-Din, a descendant of the Prophet Muhammad, and his young nephew, along with their fellow travellers, were killed by robbers in the year 764 *Hijri*. They were given a respectful burial by the local ruler, Shiv Chand. He and his descendants after him became trustees of the shrine.

187 Qasimi (p. 194) observes in his footnote to this verse that it gives the date 286, which cannot be correct, and the verse also looks incomplete.

188 Ghiyas-ud-Din Balban is credited with repairing the tomb. His grave is in Mehrauli at some distance from the *dargah* of Qutb-ud-Din Bakhtiyar Kaki.

Underneath this are inscribed the *surat Al-Ikhlas* and this *ayat* on the *mihrab* near the place where the *imam* stands:

> The Messenger believeth ... (till) ... those who stand against faith.

Panipat is an old *qasba*. In this town is the grave of Shaikh Bu 'Ali Qalandar.[189] Shaikh Bu 'Ali Qalandar came to Dehli at the age of forty. He had the privilege of meeting Hazrat Khwaja Qutb-ud-Din Bakhtiyar Kaki, and he spent twenty years in study. When he was overcome with passion for God and his heart was illumined, he threw all the books of theology into the Jamuna and set out on a journey. He went to the west and was honoured by the company of Shams-ud-Din Tabrizi, Maulana Jalal-ud-Din Rumi and other noble saints. After travelling through and visiting many countries, he came back and became a recluse in Panipat. He died in this city. The grave's entrance bears this inscription:

> The land that you blessed with your footprints,
> That land, for the believers who revere you,
> Will forever remain a place for prostration.

Towards the head of his grave, under a separate dome, is the grave of Mubariz Khan. Here there is a *dalan* with three arched openings. Its pillars are of *sang-e-mehak* [touchstone]. Here these verses are inscribed:

[1] This is a manifestation of pure light from glory and beauty, who heals and awakens the dead, like Jesus;

[2] Muqrib Khan, who is the Plato of his time; he is the son of Khan ibn-e-Khan.

[3] He is like Bu 'Ali Sina and the Aristotle of today, all look upon him in awe;

[4] He constructed a building, each pillar of which is made of heavenly sweet licorice stone

[5–6] When its date of construction was sought, it was revealed to be: 1042 [1729–30]

---

[189] A well-known Qalandariya–Chishtia Sufi; he died in 1324.

The offerings for Bu 'Ali Shah Qalandar are made up of a hundred *man* (maunds) of food, prepared from meat and curd. Outside the *dargah* is the grave of Maqrib Khan. On its headstone is written:

Allah the Almighty said, 'Despair not of the Mercy of Allah: for Allah forgives all sins: for He is Oft-Forgiving, Most Merciful.' [39:53]

In the middle of the headstone [is written]:

There is no God but Allah, and Muhammad is His Messenger.

Near it is the tomb of Shams-ud-Daulah. Above its *dalan* it says: 'It was constructed by Shams-ud-Daulah, the one with a good name.' After this is the entrance to a large square, on each side of which are doorways with *naqqar khanas*. Built by Nawab Shams-ud-Daulah Lutfullah Khan Sahib Tahawwur Jang Panipati, it is exceedingly fine and without equal. On the *dalan* is written:

Sadiq beat the drum (*naqqara*) of glory in the world, from which the date of its construction was gleaned to be 1135 [1722–23].[190]

In the environs of this *qasba* there are many other graves and tombs of the elders.

From the Lahori Gate of the *Dar-ul-Khilafa*

In front of the Lahori Gate is the old Sirhindi ki Masjid[191] and the Sarai of Mirdha Ikram.[192] The *sarai* has this chronogram inscribed on the door:

[1] During Shah Alam's reign, his esteem became well known, Sayyid says the year of construction is 1218. [1803–04]

---

[190] Lutfullah Khan was governor of Delhi at the time of Nadir Shah's invasion, and he surrendered without resistance.

[191] Sirhindi Begam was a wife of Shah Jahan, and built this mosque in 1650.

[192] Mirdha Ikram was an army officer during the reign of Shah 'Alam II, and has a family-grave enclosure close to the shrine of Nizam-ud-Din. See Zafar Hasan, Vol. 2, p. 108.

At the back of the *sarai* is the old Idgah, which is now known by the name of Shah Ganj. Shah Ganj has been established by the *kotwal* of Dehli Muhammad Hasan 'Ali Khan, son of Iradatullah Khan, son of Hafiz-ul-Mulk Nawab Hafiz Rahmatullah Khan Bahadur of Shahjahanpur, on the orders of *janab* Charles Theophilus Metcalfe Bahadur.[193] Here the road forks into two. One leads towards Pahadi Dhiraj, Teliwada, Dehli Gate, Sabzi Mandi and other areas, and the other goes towards the new Idgah. To its south is Motia Khan, i.e. there is a spring on the hill which is called Motia Khan. The water of this place is very clear and sweet. Behind this, to the west, is Habashpura, where there are the houses of the late Shidi Hamid Khan and Shidi Rehan Khan, and the garden of their father Shidi Gohar Khan. In this settlement there is also a mosque on which the following is inscribed:

> In the name of Allah who is merciful and clement. There is no God but Allah and Muhammad is his Prophet. Muhammad Shah the king, the year 24 [of his accession]. For the purpose of bestowing a reward upon Nawab Mu'izz-ud-Daulah Bahadur, Bibi Arjumand Khanam and Nawab Kazim Khan, the deceased of happy memory. Whoever should offer his prayers should invoke blessings upon the souls of these three. Whoever should accept the service of this place, there is a condition that out of the income obtained from this place during the year, he should first of all celebrate the anniversary of the death of Nawab Mu'izz-ud-Daulah on the fourteenth of the sacred month of Ramzan, of Bibi Arjmand Khanam on the seventh of the month of Safar and of the late Nawab Kazim Khan on the seventh of the month of Rajab. Should he accept the service on this condition and not act upon it, may a curse be upon him. Not for a single day must the lamp be wanting, and every Friday night he should offer prayers (for the above-mentioned deceased) with sweets and roses. The owners of this mosque and well [are] Mirza Mehdi 'Ali Khan Bahadur, son of Nawab Kazim Khan Bahadur, son of Mu'izz-ud-Daulah Bahadur, and Bibi Diyanat Nisa Khanam, mother of Mirza Mehdi 'Ali Khan, and the whole settlements [of the mosque] are at their disposal.[194]

---

[193] The *ganj* or wholesale market was evidently set up in the old Idgah.

[194] Zafar Hasan, Vol. II, p. 253. The date corresponds to 1743–44, and Zafar Hasan records this as being called Shidion ki Masjid, located within the village of Shidipura, a village probably set up by the Shidis or Indo–Africans, mentioned by Sangin Beg as living there.

After this there is a *chowki* which is known as the Badi Chowki. There is a hill near it known as Kala Pahad, where there is a temple of Shitla where Hindus perform *puja*. After this is the *sarai* of Ruhullah Khan.[195] Here there is the police *thana*, and further on, Belwada ki Chowki, Bahadurgarh, Dadri, Sanpla, Rohtak, Hansi and other places.

In the neighbourhood of the Lahori Gate of the city

To the south of this gate are a road and the old Idgah which is known as Shah Ganj. Near this is the *dargah* of Hazrat Khwaja Baqi Billah. On the southern door of the enclosure of the *dargah* is inscribed:

[1] Khwaja Baqi, that *imam* of the *auliya* [saints]. He knows the mystery of Allah and the hidden secrets.

[2] He is the perfume of the garden of the prophets. He is a happy blossom of the Ja'fri branch.

[3] For through 'annihilation' he became 'eternal', he became assimilated in the Truth and strung pearls of the secrets.

[4] He then gathered his things for the journey. He knew God's command to return.

[5] The year of the date of his *Khusrawi* union: 'he was the Naqshband of his age.' [1015/1603–04]

Inside the *dargah*, on the wall towards the head which has lamp niches, the following panegyric composed by Shah 'Abid is written:

[1] The *qibla* of spiritual persons and the Ka'ba of religious people, the object of Divine grace and the master of true knowledge,

[2] The defender of the religion of the Prophet, the most perfect leader of the pious, the recipient of the revered grace, and the descendant of the last of the prophets [Muhammad],

[3] The revealer of the supreme secrets, having knowledge of the truth ascertained by evidence, absorbed in the sacred person and faithfully firm with God,

---

[195] Ruhullah Khan's father Khalilullah Khan was married to Hamida Bano, niece of Mumtaz Mahal, the wife of Shah Jahan. The name of the village has now been corrupted to Sarai Rohilla.

[4] Ghausi A'zam [sic], having firm faith in the Lord of the universe, a *qutb* [pole star] showing the right way to the world and the signification of the true faith in God,

[5] Perfect, of excellent manner, the guide to the firm path [religion], a sea of the knowledge of God and the chief of the wise.

[6] The will and the pleasure of God is manifested through his person and disposition; this dignity is from the beloved of the Lord of the universe [the Prophet].

[7] The light of God shone on his forehead through true faith, and the hearts of the true believers were brightened by the felicity of his attention.

[8] How can I praise him, the best of the saints? The person of Khwaja Baqi is a blessing for the worlds.

[9] Baqi was a gift of God and verily he continued to be a refuge to men and angels by the grace of God.

[10] Khwajgi Amkan [sic] was the spiritual guide of that king of religion, but he belonged to the sect of Owais, and knew the secrets of religion.

[11] As his perfection was ever to have communion [with God] and its meaning was stamped on his heart, he was absorbed at last into the invisible at the age of forty.

[12] Know, the year of the death of the pole star of the age and the support of Muslims was 1012 after the flight.

[13] Whoever comes to his shrine with sincerity and belief, his desires will be fulfilled, as well as his secular and religious objects.

[14] The helpless and sinning rubs his forehead at his threshold, so that there may descend the regard of compassion, as well as salvation on the Day of Judgement.

[15] May the blessing of the Lord of the universe descend upon Muhammad Khwaja Baqi, who is one of the favoured saints.[196]

Towards the foot of the grave of Hazrat Khwaja Baqi Billah is the grave of Jan Nisar. There is a *chhatta* of his in the city. On all four sides of the headstone of the grave is written:

---

[196] Zafar Hasan, Vol. II, pp. 237–38. Khwaja Baqi Billah is a well-known Naqshbandi Sufi saint; he died in 1603.

Allah, the most Glorified is He. Hazrat Sayyid Sultan Khwaja Ahmad Peshawari, may Allah be pleased with him, Khwaja Abul Mukarim alias Jan Nisar Khan, Bahadur-e-'Alamgiri, son of Khwaja Baba son of Shah Maulana Turkistani. [1221/1806–07]

This is written on the headstone of Fatima Khanam's grave:

In the name of Allah, Most Gracious, Most Merciful.

[1]   Fatima Khanam's departure took place. She is an aspirant for the blessings and reward of Fatima.

[2]   We asked the angels about her date. They replied: 'By the name of Fatima, she is delivered'. [1184/1770–71]

Shah Nizam-ud-Din, may Allah have mercy on him, was the *subahdar* of the *Dar-ul-Khilafa* during the rule of the Marathas. At the head of his grave is the inscription:

[1]   He to whom God has given the name of Nizam-ud-Din Ahmad is the best of learned men, a perfect pole star and a great saint of his time.

[2]   He arrived in the high Paradise and Sayyid gave the year by the divine revelation, 'His place became the high Paradise'.[197]

197   Zafar Hasan, Vol. II, p. 239. The chronogram is interpreted by Zafar Hasan to give the date 1222 *Hijri* (1807–08), but Qasimi gives it as 1221 *Hijri*. See Qasimi, p. 200.

Here there is a cemetery of Musalmans in which there are the graves of 'Abdul Ahad Khan, Nawab Sulaiman Khan, and Shah 'Abid, may Allah's mercy be upon him. Here there is also a mosque made by Shah Nizam-ud-Din. The pillars of all three doors of this mosque are made of variegated stone. This kind of stone is not available in this region.

From the Khidki Farash Khana of the city wall

Facing this is a *faqir*'s *takiya* and the road to Qadam Sharif. On this road is situated a deserted mosque. Near it there used to be a garden and stepwell. At present a road passes through its midst. To its south are a cemetery and the houses of Kambalposh ascetics of the time of Muhammad Shah. Here is the *takiya* of Miyan Hasan Raza, the building of the handprint of Hazrat Imam Hussain, and the *takiya* of 'Arif Husain, the Rasul Shahi ascetic. There is a dome here under which is a grave. On the four sides of its headstone is written:

[1] They killed people pitilessly. May God save us from their murderousness! The whole world mourned that murder.

[2] The Shah who was brave in face and character, he left this world suddenly.

[3] The arrow of death pierced his head. He drank the nectar of death from the cup of martyrdom.

[4] I asked the date of his departure from intelligence. It counted and said: 'Alas, the young Husain Khan [has died]'. [947/1540–41]

On the gravestone the whole *ayat* [which begins] 'All that is on earth will perish' [55:26] is engraved, and all round the dome the names of Allah are engraved. In the adjoining field wrestling matches used to be held. They are now suspended by orders of the court due to quarrels and disputes. After this is the Kotla which was built by Emperor Firoz Shah. The details of this will be given later.

Dargah Qadam Sharif

The details of how the Qadam Sharif [blessed footprint] of the Prophet was brought here are as follows. About five hundred years ago, Makhdum Jahaniyan-e-

Jahangasht[198] brought the Qadam Sharif from the lustrous Medina. The details of this, as related in the book of the reliable teacher Ahmad Barni, are copied here:

[Verse]

[1] You were honoured through the crown and the royal throne and I from the dust on the dervish's feet.

[2] O God, give Ahmad's poor heart a place at the dervish's feet.

When Firoz, son of Rajab, became the emperor after the death of Sultan Ghiyas-ud-Din Tughlaq, he had great faith in saints and the pious. He became a spiritual disciple of Hazrat Sayyid-us-Sadat Makhdum Jahaniyan-e-Jahangasht. He troubled Hazrat Makhdum to go to the Caliph of Egypt in order to obtain the robe of *khilafat*, and sent gifts and curiosities to be presented to him. The Pole of spiritual Poles, the chief of sages, supreme among saints, lamp of the pious, sun of the mystics, best of the lovers of God, exemplar among philosophers, revelation of the mystery of God, action of the light of God, Hazrat Makhdum Jahaniyan-e-Jahangasht, set off. He travelled over sea and land, hills and plains and whatever is on this earth, performed the great Hajj seven times, and there was no such place the wonders of which he did not see and write about. He went to the extent of going to the sun in the sky and saying, 'O sun of the earth, peace be on you!' The sun answered, 'And peace be on you, O guide of the right path.' For this reason, due to the heat of the sun, his colour turned green.

When he returned from there he went to the exalted Mecca for pilgrimage, performed the Hajj, and then, travelling in a leisurely fashion, went to Medina for pilgrimage. He arrived at the Holy Shrine and asked the guards to open the door so he may perform pilgrimage of the shrine. The guards replied, 'We do not open the door except at a special time. We do however open the door for such as are of the Holy Family of the Chief of Lord's Creation, may the peace of God be upon him.' He answered, 'I am of the Holy Family of the most munificent.' They said, 'The colour of those of the family of the Prophet does not tend to be green and your colour is green.' He answered, 'The rays of the sun have turned my colour green.' They said, 'We

---

[198] The Suhrawardi Sufi saint who died in 1384.

do not accept this.' He said, 'Let all the learned, the great, the caliphs, the devout and the pious and others gather at the Holy Shrine so that the door be opened and I can enter.' When all these people gathered, each of them said three times at the Holy Shrine, 'Blessings and peace be upon you, O Prophet of God!' But none of them was honoured with an answer to that. When it was the turn of Hazrat Makhdum, he first performed his ablutions afresh, performed two *raka't namaz* and said in a loud voice, 'Blessings and peace be upon you, O Prophet of God!' The answer came from the Holy Shrine, 'And blessings and peace be upon you, O most excellent son!' After this the lock fell off the door and the door opened. Inside the Holy Shrine, when he requested the Most Munificent for a present, it was declared in the Persian tongue, 'O Makhdum-e-Jahaniyan Jahangasht, come!' When he was honoured with this title, all the people of Medina gathered and said in a loud voice, 'O Makhdum-e-Jahaniyan Jahangasht, excuse us, we did not know you.' After this they offered him many gifts but he did not accept anything. The Caliph of that place brought the footprint of Hazrat Muhammad, May the peace of God be upon him, and let him pay homage. According to the command of the Most Munificent, may the peace of God be upon him, he took the footprint of the Most Munificent with him and, accompanied by the robes of *Khilafat*, returned to Hindustan. Haji Shams-ud-Din and Haji Muhammad, who were *khadims* of the blessed footprint, also accompanied him. After some time Hazrat Makhdum arrived close to Dehli. Emperor Firoz, accompanied by the high and exalted, came 10 *kos* to welcome the footprint, and set off for Dehli bearing it on his head. When he got tired of walking, his slaves who were with him put the blessed footprint in a palanquin. He put the honoured footprint in front of him on a stand meant for a Quran and brought it to Dar-ush-Shifa which is known as Firozabad. As thanksgiving the emperor distributed a lot of money among mendicants and settled stipends on the poor. The Quran was read and the spiritual reward given to the soul of the Most Munificent. The emperor willed that after his death the blessed footprint be put on his chest.

After a year, Hazrat Makhdum dreamt that the Prophet said, 'Why have these people kept my footprint covered?' The emperor was in a quandary as to what he should do or should not do. One day, when he went out to visit the *hauz*, his grandson Fateh Khan arrived to offer salutations. The emperor was very kind to him because he was an orphan. The emperor said, 'Today you go to the treasury and whatever you like, these you bring here.' The boy went to the treasury. He saw many jewels and other things in the treasury. By chance his attention was attracted by the radiance of the holy footprint. He found out the facts. After that the prince did not take anything from the treasury and came back. The emperor asked, 'What did you choose?' The prince answered, 'The thing that I like I will bring; I hope it will be granted to me'. After that he put the holy footprint on his head and presented himself before the emperor. The emperor was astonished and said, 'Since I have become very old, it is my wish that this will be my portion. If you wish to obtain it, I put one condition, that if you die before me you get this treasure, and if I take leave of this world before you, it should be placed on my chest'. Fateh Khan was a good, pious, dutiful and very wise youth. He answered, 'Since you took my name before yours, I hope that this good fortune will be mine. It is said that when the chief of the Lord's Creation, peace be upon him, got ready to mount his horse for battle, he would enquire of an old woman, "will victory be mine or my enemy's?" The old woman used to consider the question prophetic and whichever word came to the holy tongue first, she put forward as the prophecy. I too have interpreted your words as an omen in my favour'. It occurred to the emperor, 'I am old and he is young, at this moment let me agree to this. Later we will see what will be manifest from God'. At any rate, this condition was agreed upon.

As it was fated, Prince Fateh Khan died. There was great mourning. According to the promise, the holy footprint was put on his chest, and what other relics the emperor had were also put in his grave. The emperor had a mosque, a grand *madarsa* and a big well built, and had an enclosing wall built around these. Whatever holy water of Zamzam remained with the emperor was put into this well. A stone utensil was made in which ten *maunds* of sugar-candy *sharbat* used to be made, and a lot of food used to be prepared. The Sultan ordered that food should be given daily to the people. Fifty-two villages and a piece of land, which was called Zareeh Khas and was composed of many plots of agricultural land, were endowed in *waqf* for this tomb. The details of several of these plots of land are present in the *Farman-e-Firozi*. The seals of several great *'ulama*, saints, judges of Islamic law and various noblemen of Hazrat Dehli are affixed on the *waqfnama* (the deed of endowment). This *waqfnama* was prepared and handed over to the *khuddam* in the month of Safar, 709 *Hijri* [1309–10]. The signature of the polestar of the learned, Makhdum Jahaniyan, can also be seen on this *waqfnama* at a separate spot. The emperor himself put his signature on it, and, on the wishes of the prince's mother, appointed the teacher of the prince, the learned and virtuous Hafiz Maulana Shah Amin, as teacher and trustee. He was ordered to distribute the income of the *waqf* with advice and serve as trustee. After this Emperor Firoz lived twenty-three years and finally departed for the next world on the thirteenth of Ramzan 790 *Hijri* [1388]. He was buried beside the above-mentioned *hauz*. In several histories Fateh Khan is mentioned as the elder son of Firoz Shah.[199] After Firoz Shah, Fateh Khan's son Tughlaq Shah became emperor for a while. This Tughlaq Shah is different from Ghiyas-ud-Din Tughlaq Shah and Muhammad Tughlaq Shah the tyrant, who is known as 'Adil [the Just]. Only Allah is wise.

On the third doorway of the *dargah* Qadam Sharif, which is attached to the Naqqar Khana, it is written in golden letters:

[1] The guide of those who have lost their way is Muhammad; the director of directors is Muhammad.

[2] Glorious are the school, the pulpit and the court where there is read the praise of Muhammad.

---

[199] Fateh Khan was indeed the son of Firoz Shah. The story of the footprint is somewhat controversial within the Sufi tradition.

[3] For the broken-hearted he is a balm, for the hearts of the afflicted he is medicine.

[4] The sky becomes secure under the feet of him who has become a beggar of Muhammad.

[5] I am one of the dogs of his lane, and Shirwan has become a beggar of Muhammad.

Alias Shirwan Khan, the son of Raihan Khan, the Abyssinian, wrote these lines on the twenty-third of Rabi'-us-Sani of the year 1082 [29 August 1671].[200]

Surrounding the auspicious footprint, in the shape of a tank, is an enclosure of marble. This tank is always full of sugar, milk, water and flowers. People drink this water in the form of a benediction.

[Couplet]

[1] O Khizr of the heart, salvation lies in drinking this water.
The water of the Qadam Sharif is the water of life.

Here are the graves of the elders. Outside it, adjacent to the mosque, is a *bangla* on which is written '*Khuld-e-Sani*' [the second paradise]. Near the *bangla* is a grave. On it grows a tamarind tree, on whose branches are glass bangles of the sort women wear. The reason for this is that those in need pray for their wishes to come true and through God's mercy and favour, their prayers are granted. Upon this, they offer food prepared from rice and sets of bangles. Near the Naqqar Khana is the grave of Shah 'Abdullah Bukhari. Outside the Kotla,[201] towards the city, are the Talab-e-Firoz, the Muslim graveyard and the Kali Masjid. The *sihraha* of Qadam Sharif was constructed by Khan-e-Jahan. Inside it is written, 'There is no God but Allah, and Muhammad is His Messenger'. From the first to the twelfth of Rabi'-ul-Awwal,[202] people gather at the *dargah* of Qadam Sharif. *Faqirs* come from near and far for twelve days, and sell cornelian and turquoise here.

---

[200] Zafar Hasan, Vol. II, p. 242.

[201] The *dargah* was enclosed in a small fortification or *kotla*.

[202] A period in the Islamic calendar during which the birth and death of Prophet Muhammad are commemorated.

Near the Ajmeri Gate is the *madarsa* of the late Ghazi-ud-Din Khan.[203] Behind this are the tombs of Nawab Amin-ud-Din Khan and his son Nawab Qamar-ud-Din Khan. Nawab Qamar-ud-Din Khan was the *wazir* of Emperor Muhammad Shah. The two graves are on a marble platform. On the headstone of Nawab Amin-ud-Din Khan's grave, on all four sides, this is inscribed:

Allah is He, than Whom there is no other God; – the Sovereign, the Holy One, the Source of Peace (and Perfection), the Guardian of Faith, the Preserver of Safety, the Exalted in Might, the Irresistible, the Supreme; Glory to Allah! (High is He) above the partners they attribute to Him. [59:23–24] Allah and His angels send blessings on the Prophet: O ye that believe! Send ye blessings on him, and salute him with all respect. [33:56]

There is no God but Allah, and Muhammad is His Messenger. O Most Gracious, Most Merciful! O [Thou] full of Majesty and Honour! O Exalter! O Intercessor! O All Hearing! O Bountiful One! O All Knowing! O Forbearing One!

---

[203] This *madarsa* was built in the late seventeenth century by Ghazi-ud-Din Khan, who was a high-ranking nobleman during the reign of Aurangzeb, and the father of Asaf Jah. In 1825 this *madarsa* came to house Delhi College, the first western-style college in Delhi. The Delhi College was later renamed Zakir Husain College, which has now moved to a new location. The Ghazi-ud-Din *madarsa* building now houses the Anglo–Arabic school.

Allah! There is no God but He, – the Living, the Self-subsisting, Eternal. No slumber can seize Him nor sleep. His are all things in the heavens and on earth. Who is there can intercede in His presence except as He permitteth? He knoweth what (appeareth to His creatures as) before or after or behind them. Nor shall they compass aught of His knowledge except as He willeth. His Throne doth extend over the heavens and the earth, and He feeleth no fatigue in guarding and preserving them for He is the Most High, the Supreme (in glory). [2:255]

[1] From dust of the darkness of being ran the colour of eternity. How can one trust the passing of time?

[2] From morning to evening the sun raises high the flags of the faith of Muhammad.

[3] As his pure spirit has gone to heaven, it has taken the place there of the head of the assembly of the honoured spirits.

[4] Intelligence tells the date of his death in this way: 'He was the Shah's representative, a defender of Islam.' [1133/1720–21]

[1] I'timad-ud-Daulah, who is the law of his times, ornamented the faith and went towards heaven.

[2] His soul united with the mercy of God, and this is the date of his death. [1133/1720–21]

Qit'a [couplet sequence]

[1] O Lord, by the honour of the Messenger, of Abu Bakr and 'Umar, 'Usman and Haidar.

[2] Of the Messenger's daughter and the two sons, spare this place on the Day of the Gathering.

(Engraved by Muhammad Afzal)

Sideways, towards the side, is written [in Arabic]: 'May Allah forgive me my sins.'

After this is Kotle ki Mandi, the *madarsa* of Maulvi Fakhr-ud-Din Sahib, shops of grocers, Jahangir Ganj, the shop of Tek Chand, Pan ki Mandi and the *chowki* of royal soldiers who do guard duty. Outside the gate of the above-named *ganj* is the Shah Ganj, which is called Pahad Ganj. Here there is the Panwariyon ka Mohalla, Sabzi Mandi,

Khand ki Mandi, Sabun ki Mandi, Gur ki Mandi and other *muhallas*.[204] There are shops of grocers, shops of Kishan Chand Sarraf and other artisans. There is also a *baoli* and the building of the police *sarkar* which is connected to Sarai Basant. This has recently been constructed from stone and brick through the efforts of Rup Chand Pandit, a *sipahi* of the *thana*, I think, under the orders of the court. Near this is a fortified stone enclosure. In earlier times the Karor ki Kachehri was located here. Then there is the Muhalla Maltola, Muhalla Khati Laddu, Katra Basdeo Zanjabeel and other localities, and Misri Khan ka Phatak. Here there are houses of the people and the *dargah* of Hazrat Sayyid Hasan Rasul Numa. His *'urs* is on the twenty-second day of Shaban. On the enclosure wall of the *dargah* is written:

> His name is Hasan Rasul Numa and he is the pride of the lineage of Husain; he, the second Owais-e-Qurni and the third Hasnain. [1103/1692–93]

Behind this, in the north, is the *takiya* of a *faqir* and Panchkuiyan. There is also a road that leads to Motia Khan and a hill. On this hill is a site that is known as 'Mohull-e-Bola', but it is popularly called Boli Bhatiyari ka Mahal. In various histories this has been described as the palace of Deval Rani, whose tale is famous in books.[205] Here, in the beginning of the month of *Bhadon*, on the third day, standards of the Salonas are set up and people of the city come to see this. The sweepers and *jogis* of the city also set up standards of Goga, i.e. Lal Beg. People collect here for three days.

Towards the south is Kalali Bagh, where Mewati labourers live.[206] After this is the garden of Muhammad Yar Khan and at the foot of the hill, the Shahi Tal Katora Bagh. After this is the settlement of Jai Singh Pura.[207] In its neighbourhood is the Parasnath temple of the Saraogis built by Sukh Chand Mahajan. Here there is the Manpidharath Talab. Near this settlement to the east is Hanumanji ka Mandir, a *baoli*, and a general *chowki*. There is an observatory called Jantar Mantar, which was constructed by A'la Hazrat 'Firdaus

---

[204] Panwariyon ka Mohalla, i.e. neighbourhood of betel-leaf dealers; the named *mandis* are for vegetables, raw sugar, soap and jaggery, respectively.

[205] This is now believed to be a hunting lodge constructed by Firoz Shah Tughlaq.

[206] In the twentieth century this area was redeveloped as housing in the vicinity of Gole Market.

[207] This is the area adjoining Jantar Mantar, which still has a road named after Jai Singh, the ruler of Amer.

Aramgah' Muhammad Shah.[208] This emperor is the compiler of the modern Muhammad Shahi astronomical tables. Mir Khairullah prepared them. The common people say that Raja Jai Singh of Jainagar made the observatory from the above-mentioned tables in the service of Emperor Muhammad Shah in order to tell the time.[209] 'Only Allah is wise.' Near the Jantar Mantar is a temple of the Hindus where twice a year, at an interval of six months, a *mela* of three days duration is held and people of the city gather.[210]

There is a fork in the road from Jai Singh Pura. One goes towards Rakab Ganj, where there is the *dera* of the Guru of the Sikhs.[211] This road goes to Malcha, Sarai Basant, Mahram Nagar and Sarai Sambhal, where his grave is also located. The same road also goes to *mauza-e-Bijwasan*, Chaumoth, Sarai Allahwardi, and *mauza-e-Gurgaon*. Gurgaon is located at a distance of 12 *kos* from Dehli. After this is the *garhi* of Sirsa. At a distance of 2 *kos* from here is *mauza-e-Pataudi*. From here at a distance of 8 *kos* is Rewari. At a distance of 3 *kos* from here is the cantonment, the *bangla* of the judge of the southern district, *kothis* of other high British officials, and the camp of the English battalion. The other road from Jai Singh Pura leads to Khwaja Qutb-ud-Din Sahib.

Outside the Turkman Gate
Close to the city wall is the grave of 'Ali Shah and the garden of Hazrat Shah Nizam-ud-Din,[212] which is at present lying waste. Here are also the tombs of Khwaja Nasir and Khwaja Mir Dard. The grave of Khwaja Nasir bears this:

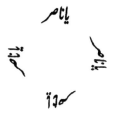

---

208   'Resting in paradise': the posthumous title of Emperor Muhammad Shah.

209   Raja Jai Singh, an avid astronomer, had a much greater role in formulating the structures than Sangin Beg gives him credit for.

210   The Hanuman temple on Baba Kharak Singh Marg.

211   The Rakab Ganj gurudwara.

212   The governor during Maratha rule.

O Allah, send blessings and peace upon Muhammad and his family!

[1] Khwaja Muhammad Nasir is beloved of God; Khwaja Muhammad Nasir shows the way to truth.

[2] Khwaja Muhammad Nasir is a leader, an intercessor and a supporter of all in both worlds.

Nasir-ul-Mulk wad-Din, the chief of the true Muhammadis, Muhammadi, having the poetic name 'Andalib, may the blessings be upon him. Born in the month of Shaban – Heir of the knowledge of Imams and 'Ali – 1105 [1693]. Died on Saturday after the third prayer; at eventide, second of the month of Sha'ban, 1172 [31 March 1759], at the honourable age of sixty-six.[213]

The words 'O Nasir'[214] are also inscribed on the grave in *tughra*.

The grave of Khwaja Mir Dard has the following inscription:

The light [son] of Nasir, the first of the Muhammadis, Khwaja Mir 'Ali Muhammadi, whose poetic name is Dard, may the blessings of God be upon him, his parents, and those who are connected with him. Born on Tuesday the nineteenth of Zi-Qad of the year 1133 [11 September 1721]. At the honourable age of sixty-six, died on Friday, the twenty-fourth of Safar before the dawn of day, in the year 1199 [6 January 1785].

The phrase in *tughra* is:

O Nasir, may Allah aid us and bless us with benedictions.

[1] Khwaja Mir Dard has a conscience [as bright as] the sun. Khwaja Mir Dard is also [like] the bright full moon.

[2] Khwaja Mir Dard is a chief, though a beggar. Khwaja Mir Dard is a guide and a leader.[215]

---

[213] Zafar Hasan, Vol. II, p. 67. Muhammad Nasir was the father of Mir Dard.

[214] 'O Helper', one of the 99 names of Allah.

[215] Zafar Hasan, Vol. II, pp. 67–68.

May Allah the Exalted be pleased with him and may the two be pleased with him. Amen.

The inscription on the headstone of Khwaja Mir Asar's grave:

[1] As we are the slaves of Khwaja Mir, O Asar! We are beneath the feet of Khwaja Mir, O Asar!

[2] By the blessing of God we shall have eternal life whenever we die with the name of the Khwaja.[216]

To Allah we belong, and to Him is our return. We are content with His contentment. We abide in His reunion.

Towards the side of the grave, on a red-stone plate, is inscribed:

He is the Protector [Al-Nasir]

[1] This is blessed ground. May it always be pure. May it be the envy of the highest sphere, the stars and the skies.

[2] For this reason his honoured exaltedness is here: the gift of his footprint is here.

[3] Fate is elevated by his perfection. Vision is made noble by his beauty.

[4] Men are improved by his qualities. Pray for him and his family.

On the arch of the mosque is written:

Equal to the *qibla-e-haqiqi* and the *ka'ba-e-tahqiqi*. [1204/1789–90]

Between Turkman Gate and Dehli Gate, on the outside, is the tomb of Nawab Ghazi-ud-Din Khan,[217] the *haveli* of Khwaja Basit, the *baoli* of Miyan Rajji, and amidst the ruins of a dome is the Dalao ka Takiya [literally, hermitage of the rubbish heap] and *thaan*. In the middle of this is the grave of Shaikh Muhammad 'Ali. Because there are ruins here, this hermitage has been named the hermitage of the rubbish heap. There

---

216 Ibid., p. 68. Mir Asar was the younger brother of Mir Dard.

217 The tomb of Ghazi-ud-Din Khan is actually in the *madarsa* complex outside Ajmeri Gate.

are buildings here that are known by the name of Mehndiyan. In this are the tomb of Shaikh 'Abdul 'Aziz Shakarbar and other buildings. There is also the cemetery of Shah Waliullah Sahib, the glorious father of Hazrat Shah 'Abdul 'Aziz Sahib. In this cemetery are the graves of Maulvi Rafi'-ud-Din Sahib and Maulvi 'Abdul Qadir Sahib.[218] There is the jail for prisoners sentenced by the Faujdari 'Adalat [criminal court] and the Lal Darwaza of Old Dehli. Near this is the Firoz Shah Kotla where a stone pillar stands. Such letters are inscribed on this pillar as no one in this district can read. In addition, words from the *Shastra* are also inscribed on this pillar. To the extent that it can be read, this is the translation:

> Bikramajit sammat [sic] 1240, the month of Baisakh, Monday the fifteenth, written on a Monday. Bishan Das Narayan Shah Bahadur Mu'in-ud-Din, he himself is the standard of nobility.

The letters are inscribed in this manner:

ع ٦٨ ٤٦٩٤٨ ﭼﭖ ٦ر ٦٨٨ ٨٨ ٨ٮ ٨٧٤ ٦٣٦ﭼ پٰ٦ س

The history of the above-mentioned stones, denominated the Firoz Shah ki Lath, is as follows. Both these stones were lying close to Kumaon, a mountain of north India. It was widely believed by the Hindus that one of their *avatars*, whose name is not known, held these in his hand instead of a stick to herd his cattle. After his death the Hindus used to go to worship these stones; they came from far and wide, and gathered together as in the Haridwar fair. They used to say that if these stones were lifted or moved by anybody, a minor doomsday would be manifested. Hearing this and wanting to prove this conjecture wrong, Firoz Shah moved these stones, which had broken in places due to earthquakes, from their place and put one in the above-mentioned Kotla, where it still stands.[219]

---

[218] The eighteenth-century Islamic scholar Shah Waliullah and his sons.

[219] For the correct explanation for the pillar, see Firoz Shah's pillars, as mentioned above. The date inscribed is from a later inscription on the pillar.

From early times till the reign of Firoz Shah, clocks were not in use. Other emperors had devised seven things such as the crown and the throne. The eighth thing, the clock, was invented by Firoz Shah. Otherwise there was no such gauge by which the rays of the sun could be measured.[220]

After this, in the sands, is the *haveli* of Mahabat Khan. After this is the *gumti* of Khizr Khan. Here, towards the east, the tomb of Shaikh Muhammad is located. On the entrance to this tomb is written:

[1] The pole star of his times, this *sarai* is of Shaikh Muhammad: He who took his heart away and set off for the world to come.

[2] And the date of his effacement in the union with Truth: the union of the lover and beloved . . . [221]

At a distance of 1 *kos* from here is the Purana Qil'a. Its foundation was laid during the reign of Emperor Babur and it was completed during the reign of Emperor Humayun.[222]

---

[220] This is obviously a historically inaccurate statement.

[221] Qasimi notes that since the last word of this chronogram is illegible, its date cannot be ascertained. See Qasimi, p. 213, fn 3.

[222] In fact the foundations too were laid during Humayun's reign.

Its name is Dinpanah. During the reign of Sher Shah too there was construction here. Here, close to the mosque, there is a tower which the common people call 'Sher Mandal'. But this is not Sher Mandal. The facts are this: that Emperor Humayun had it built in order to observe the star Canopus and other stars. One day, when he had gone to the roof of this building to look at Canopus, the call to the evening prayer came to his ears. In order to honour the call the emperor tried to get up by leaning on his staff, but it so happened that the cloak he was wearing got entangled in his feet, and he fell from the roof and died. The famous chronogram of his death is: 'The emperor Humayun fell from the roof' [962/1554–55].

There are five arched entrances in the congregational mosque located in the fort. On the middle three, the following is engraved. Towards the south, over the first entrance, the complete *surat Al-Mulk* in the Sulus script. On the second entrance, which is in the middle and larger than the two entrances beside it, the *surat* 'Verily we have granted a victory':

> In the name of Allah, Most Gracious, Most Merciful. Verily we have granted thee a manifest victory: That Allah may forgive thee thy faults of the past. [48:1–2]

Towards the north, above the third entrance, the complete *surat Al-Muzammil*.

There are five *mihrabs* in the mosque. Above the first *mihrab*, the *surat Al-Baqara* till 'they do not believe' and the complete *surat* 'Seest thou one who...' [*surat Al-Ma'un*] are inscribed. Inside the *mihrab* is written:

> In the name of Allah, Most Gracious, Most Merciful. Say: O Allah! Lord of Power (and Rule), Thou givest power to whom Thou pleasest, and Thou strippest off power from whom Thou pleasest: Thou endowest with honour whom Thou pleasest, and Thou bringest low whom Thou pleasest: In Thy hand is all good. Verily, over all things Thou hast power. [3:26] And Allah hath full power and control over His affairs; but most among mankind know it not. [12:21]

On the right-hand side is written: 'O the Revealer'. On the left-hand side: 'O Allah'.

Above the second *mihrab*, in the Sulus script, the *surat Al-Jumu'ah* is written till 'That is best for you if ye but knew!' [*ayat* 9] Inside the second *mihrab*, in the Sulus script, the *surat* 'Say: I seek refuge with the Lord of the Dawn' [*surat Al-Falaq*], and the *surat* 'Say: I seek refuge with the Lord and Cherisher of Mankind' [*surat Al-Nas*]; and under this in the Kufic script is written: 'There is no God but Allah, and Muhammad is His Messenger. Glory be to Allah.' Under this are the *surat Al-Ikhlas* and the *kalima-e-tayyib*. And under it is written: 'As long as the world is populated, may this edifice be frequented and may the people of the world be cheerful and happy in it.'[223] On both sides the names of Allah are written.

Above the third *mihrab*, the *surat Al-Yasin* till the first '*mubin*' [*ayat* 12] is written. Inside the *mihrab* is written:

> To Allah belongeth all that is in the heavens and on earth. Whether ye show what is in your minds or conceal it, Allah calleth you to account for it. He forgiveth whom He pleaseth, and punisheth whom He pleaseth, for Allah hath power over all things. [2:284]

Under this the *surat Al-Fatiha*, and under that the *kalima-e-tayyib* and a name of Allah [are written].

Under the dome, a golden goblet or bowl is suspended. Above the *mihrab* of the fourth entrance, the *surat* 'Verily we have granted thee a victory' till 'Full of knowledge and wisdom' [48:1–4] is written. Within it [is written]: 'His Domain. O Thou Opener.' Under this:

> There is a mosque whose foundation was laid from the first day on piety; it is more worthy of the standing forth (for prayer) therein. In it are men who love to be purified; and Allah loveth those who make themselves pure. [9:108]

After this:

> There is no God but He: That is the witness of Allah, His angels, and those endued with knowledge, standing firm on justice. There is no God but He, the Exalted in Power, the Wise. The Religion before Allah is Islam. [3:18–19]

---

[223] Zafar Hasan, Vol. II, p. 98.

Below this [is written] the *surat Al-An'am* (till 'ye doubt within yourselves') [6:1–2]. And below it the *ayat Al-Kursi* (till 'the Most High, the Supreme') [is written]. Below it 'His Domain' is written in the *tughra* style. After this the *kalima-e-tayyib* and 'Glory to Allah' are written in the Kufic script, and below them the *surat Al-Ikhlas* is written. Below this the following quatrain is written:

> [1] O God! Show mercy for we are polluted, and our liver is washed with the blood of our heart.
>
> [2] Instruct us as is best in thy sight for we have been wanting in our duties.[224]

Under this [is written] the *kalima-e-tayyib*: 'There is no God but Allah, and Muhammad is His Messenger.' Below this on both sides is written: 'Allah sufficeth for me.'

The *ayat* above the fifth *mihrab* [is] 'Had ee sent down this Quran on a mountain, verily, Thou wouldst have seen it humble itself' till the *ayat* 'and He is the Exalted in Might, the Wise' [59:20–24]. Below this the complete *surat* 'Seest thou not how' is written [105]. Inside the *mihrab* is written the complete *surat* 'Say: O ye that reject Faith' [109]. And below it: 'There is no God but Allah, and Abraham is a friend of Allah. O Allah. O [the] Opener.'

At a distance of half a *kos* to the east of the above-mentioned fort, near the garden of Sayyid Mir Khan, son of Shah Nizam-ud-Din, is a tomb which is known as Sundri. Here, under the dome, the following couplet is engraved in the Sulus script:

> [1] It is better that the face of my grave after my death remain desolate.
>
> [2] A wretched one like me is happier under dust, desolate.

This is the tomb of some Chaghtai prince. To the west of the fort is the mosque of Akbar Shah. The following is inscribed on its central arch: 'In the name of Allah, Most Gracious, Most Merciful', and the *ayat* 'Glory to Allah Who' till the *ayat* 'for those who reject all Faith' [17:1–8]. Below this, inside the above-mentioned *mihrab*, the following chronogram is engraved:

---

224 Ibid., p. 98.

[1]   In the time of Jalaluddin Muhammad who is the greatest [Akbar] of just kings,

[2]   When Maham Beg the protection of chastity, erected this building for the virtuous,

[3]   Shihab-ud-din Ahmad Khan, the generous, assisted [in the erection of] this good house.

[4]   How blessed is this good building that its chronogram is 'best of houses'.
Composed by Niyaz Bakhsh under the supervision of Darvesh Husain [225]

On both sides the *kalima-e-tayyib* is written in a circular pattern. Inside the mosque, where the *pesh imam* stands, this is written:

> He is Allah; there is no God but He. He is the Knower of the Unseen and Visible; He is Most Merciful, Most Compassionate. (The complete *ayat Al-Kursi*)

On both sides:

> The Domain of Allah.

From here one road goes towards Shahjahanabad which is known at the Rasta-e-Rarha. On this road is the grave of Fatima Saam.[226] Near the Lal Darwaza of Old Dehli is the grave of Nur-ud-Din Malik Yar Paran. He died on the eighteenth of Jamadi-ul-Akhir 681 *Hijri* [1282].[227] Here, in the Bijay Mandal, is the grave of Shaikh Hasan Tahir. He died in 909 *Hijri* [1503–04].[228] Near this Mandal is the grave of Mirza Shah Muhammad Jamali. He died in 924 *Hijri* [1518–19]. Near the same gate is the grave of Shaikh Hasan. The date of his death is 967 *Hijri* [1559–60]. Close to the gate mentioned above [Lal

---

[225] Ibid., p. 52. The mosque and *madarsa*, known as Khair-ul-Manazil, were built by Maham Anga, who had been the wet nurse of Akbar. The chronogram is worked out as 969 *Hijri*, i.e. 1561–62 (Qasimi, p. 217).

[226] Bibi Fatima Saam was a Sufi revered by Nizam-ud-Din Auliya. She died in 1246–47, and her *dargah* is in Kaka Nagar.

[227] Nur-ud-Din Malik Yar Parran was a Sufi. His grave is in Bagh-e-Bedil, next to the National Sports Club of India. The Lal Darwaza is located close to Khair-ul-Manazil.

[228] Though Sangin Beg locates this grave here, today another grave, close to the Bijay Mandal monument in south Delhi, is identified as that of Hasan Tahir.

Darwaza] is the grave of Abu Bakr Tusi Haidari. He died in 878 Hijri [1473–74].[229] In Old Dehli is the grave of Mardan Khan Habshi. From Khwaja Qutb-ud-Din to Faridabad, opposite the Kashmiri Gate of the *Dar-ul-Khilafa*, is located the famous Old Dehli.[230] Near the Purana Qil'a, on the road to Hazrat Nizam-ud-Din Auliya, is a mosque. On its entrance is engraved the following chronogram in verse:

[1] In the time of Shah Gharib Nawaz, who is the refuge of the faith and of pure breath.

[2] Who is the king of the stars and the leader of emperors, and the world is only adorned by him.

[3] A special slave of the exalted *khan*, Mukarramat Khan, patron for all.

[4] Constructed from that fortunate, angelic extraction, a mosque like the crystalline dome [of God]

[5] The year of its beginning comes from the unknown: the room of the Ka'ba, the holiest *qibla*. [1055/1645–46]

Adjacent to this is the tomb of princes, which is famous as the Lal Bangla.[231] After this is a broken gateway. And after this, Dehli's Ghiyaspura, the tombs of Hazrat Nizam-ud-Din Auliya, Amir Khusro[232] and some Afghan nobles of this era. Inside the entrance to the enclosure of the *dargah* is written in golden letters: 'How rare are kings who give to beggars.' In here there is a stepwell constructed by Hazrat Nizam-ud-Din Auliya. Near the gateway to the *dargah* is a dome with tile-work. Within it is written on the tiles:

[1] O faithful! This was not faithfulness, nor was this the custom of friendship with friends,

[2] You gave up all regard for me and went away, you threw me into the dust and blood and went away.

---

[229] The shrine is today known as that of Matka Pir. The Haideri Qalandari saint actually lived in the thirteenth century, so the date given is incorrect.

[230] This is a confusing statement, for which no explanation can be hazarded.

[231] Lal Bangla is now in the Delhi Golf Course.

[232] Amir Khusro (1253–1325) was a nobleman, a beloved disciple of Nizam-ud-Din Auliya, and an extremely gifted poet and musician.

[3] What a wonderful thorn you have broken in my heart that it does not issue until I am reduced to dust.

[4] You have set fire to the straw of my person from which wreaths of smoke ascend to heaven.

[5] No one opened his eyes in my smoke, but from his eye dropped fire.[233]

Quatrain

[1] Because of you in my heart there is sadness and sadness. May you always be happy and be happy at all times.

[2] May the rite of happiness progress. And may the thought of union enter your thoughts.

Quatrain

[1] By the grace of God's benevolence I hid my heart and departed. I told no one of my heart's secret and departed.

[2] I was like a bird that lives in a cage in this world. I broke this cage and departed. [921/1515–16]

The grave of the *haram* [wife/concubine] of Muhammad Shah is situated in a canopy-like marble dome. At its side, on the headstone, is written:

O Allah. O Most Gracious One. O Most Merciful One. O Lord. O Pure One. O Source of Peace. O Inspirer of Faith. O Guardian. O Victorious One. O Compeller.

On the eastern side of the headstone:

O Greatest One. O Creator. O the Maker of Order. O Forgiving One. O Subduer. O Giver of All. O Provider. O Opener. O Knower of All. O Constrictor. O Forgiver of Faults. O Rewarder of Thankfulness. O Greatest One. O Preserver. O Sustainer. O 'Ali. O Mighty One. O Generous One. O Watchful One. O All-Comprehending.

---

[233] Zafar Hasan, Vol. II, p. 141. The building is known as Cheeni ka Burj. By the time Zafar Hasan recorded the inscription, much of it had been obliterated. Sangin Beg recorded all of it and added the date 921 *Hijri*.

O Majestic One. O Perfectly Wise. O Resurrector. O Witness. O Truth. O Trustee.
O Possessor of All Strength. O Forceful One. O Praised One. O Governor.

On the western side of the headstone:

O Restorer. O Life-Giver. O Originator. O Concealed One. O Expediter. O Delayer.
O Ever-Living One. O Self-Existing One. O Finder. O Glorious One. O the One.
O Satisfier of All Needs. O All Powerful. O Creator of All Power. O First. O Last.
O Manifest One. O Hidden One. O Protecting Friend. O Supreme One. O Righteous
One. O Rewarding One. O Generous One. O Avenger. O Clement One. O Owner of All.
O Lord of Majesty and Bounty. O Gatherer. O Rich One. O Preventer of Harm.
O Creator of Good. O Innovator. O Corrector. O Supreme Heir. O Most Patient One.
O Appointer of the Path. O Full of Truth. O Enricher. O Giver. O Everlasting One.
O Guide. O Pardoner. O Veiler.

At the foot of the headstone, on both sides [is written]:

[1] I enquired of the heart, which is pure and of innocent disposition, the year of
her death.
[2] It heaved a deep sigh, and told me to say, 'May she be a companion of the *houris*
of paradise'. [1080/1669–70]
Bai Kokaldai, daughter of Mulayam Khan.

On the top of the headstone [is written]: 'Say: O my Servants who have transgressed
against their souls! Despair not of the Mercy of Allah' till the end of the *ayat* [39:53].

The inscriptions at the mosque of Hazrat Nizam-ud-Din Auliya
Towards the south, above the first entrance [is written]: 'In the name of Allah, Most
Gracious, Most Merciful. Glory to Allah Who did take His servant for a journey by night
from the Sacred Mosque to the farthest Mosque' till 'it was a warning completely
fulfilled' [17:1–5]. In the middle doorway of the mosque is a latticed *mihrab* with this *ayat*:

Say: 'O my Lord! Let my entry be by the Gate of Truth and Honour, and likewise my exit by the Gate of Truth and Honour; and grant me from Thy Presence an authority to aid (me)! [17:80]

Above the large middle entrance the *surat Al-Rahman* is written till 'Then which of the favours of your Lord will ye deny?' [55:1–16] Below this on the *mihrab* is written: 'In the name of Allah. Say: "O Allah! Lord of Power and Rule"' till the *ayat* 'Thou givest sustenance to whom Thou pleasest, without measure' [3:26–27]. Towards the south, on the side of the entrance, on a latticed screen is written: 'In the name of Allah. There is no God but He: That is the witness of Allah, His angels, and those endued with knowledge, standing firm on justice. There is no God but He, the Exalted in Power, the Wise.' [3:18] Next to it is engraved the chronogram giving the date of death of the honourable Nizam of Truth and Faith:

[1] The administrator [Nizam] of two worlds, the king of water and earth surely became a lamp for both the worlds.

[2] When I sought the date of his death from the invisible, the invisible crier said, 'the emperor of religion'.[234]

Above the third entrance the *surat* 'Verily we have granted a victory' till the *ayat* 'and Allah is Full of Knowledge and Wisdom' [48:1–4] is written. Under the rounded dome in sixteen circles the *kalima-e*-tayyib is engraved. Below this the 99 names of the Exalted Truth [Allah] are engraved in this fashion:

Allah is He, than Whom there is no other God; the Sovereign, the Holy One, the Source of Peace. [59:23]
The Granter of Security. The Protector. The Mighty. The Compeller. The Majestic. The Creator. The Maker. The Shaper. The Forgiver. The Subduer. The Bestower. The Provider. The Withholder. The Forgiving. The Veiler. The Expander. The Preserver.

Below this around the place between the place where the *pesh imam* stands and the

---

[234] Zafar Hasan, Vol. II, p. 152. This is a chronogram of the date of death of Nizam-ud-Din Auliya, i.e. 725 *Hijri* [1325]. The mosque is known as Jama'at Khana, and was built during 'Ala-ud-Din's reign.

mihrab are written four *ruku*'s of the *surat Al-An'am* till the *ayat* 'He would remove the distress which occasioned your call upon Him, and ye would forget the false gods which ye join with Him' [6:41]. Below this is written the *surat Al-Mulk* till the *ayat* 'and evil is such Destination' [67:6]. Below it, where the *pesh imam* stands, [is written] in the Sulus script, on the *mihrab*:

> In the name of Allah, Most Gracious, Most Merciful. The first House (of worship) appointed for men was that at Bakka: Full of blessing and of guidance for all kinds of beings: In it are Signs Manifest; (for example), the Station of Abraham; whoever enters it attains security; Pilgrimage thereto is a duty men owe to Allah, those who can afford the journey; but if any deny faith, Allah stands not in need of any of His creatures. Say: 'O People of the Book! Why reject ye the Signs of Allah, when Allah is Himself witness to all ye do?' [3:96–98]

Below this [are written] the complete *surat*, 'We have indeed revealed this Message' [*surat Al-Qadr*] and the *kalima*, 'There is no God but Allah, and Muhammad is His Messenger'. Towards the north, above the *mihrab* [is written] the *surat Al-Ikhlas* and below it the Holy Hadith:

> There is no God but Allah, and Muhammad is His Messenger. The Messenger of Allah, may Allah bless him and his family and bring peace on him, said, 'he who constructs a mosque, Allah will construct a house like it for him in paradise'.

From the centre of the dome a golden goblet or bowl is suspended. In this mosque, on a door adjoining the western wall, is an opening. From here the air enters and this is called the 'breeze of paradise'. Under the canopy of the *dargah* of Hazrat Nizam-ud-Din Auliya, on the headstone, is written in golden lettering:

> There is no God but Allah and Muhammad is His Prophet.
> [1] Thanks [be to God] that the Khan of the dignity of the sky resolved to build the tomb of His Holiness, the Ghaus of the world [Shaikh Nizam-ud-Din].
> [2] He [the Khan] is the glory of the sun of [his] family and a star of the height of honour, a Sayyid of high descent and a chief of the standing of a king.

[3] Its [the tomb's] founder was a Hashimi [a descendant of Hashim, the ancestor of the Prophet Muhammad] and its builder was a Hashimi, men in whose time flourished poetry and prose.

[4] When I sought to discover its date, the pen of wisdom wrote 'Qiblagah of nobles and commoners' [i.e. all] [970/1562–63]

[5] O Faridun! Turn your face with truth towards his tomb, perchance by the favours of the saint your work may be accomplished.

The scribe of this: Husain Ahmad Chishti.[235]

On the western wall [is written]:

Allah! There is no God but He – the Living, the Self-subsisting, Eternal. No slumber can seize Him nor sleep. His are all things in the heavens and on earth. Who is there can intercede in His presence except as He permitteth? He knoweth what (appeareth

---

[235] Ibid., p. 146. The several additions to the grave were made by various devotees over time.

to His creatures as) before or after or behind them. Nor shall they compass aught of His knowledge except as He willeth. His Throne doth extend over the heavens and the earth, and He feeleth no fatigue in guarding and preserving them for He is the Most High, the Supreme (in glory).[236]

Below it:

Establish regular prayers – at the sun's decline till the darkness of the night, and the morning prayer and reading: for the prayer and reading in the morning carry their testimony. And pray in the small watches of the morning: (it would be) an additional prayer (or spiritual profit) for thee: soon will thy Lord raise thee to a Station of Praise and Glory! Say: 'O my Lord! Let my entry be by the Gate of Truth and Honour, and likewise my exit by the Gate of Truth and Honour; and grant me from Thy Presence an authority to aid (me)'. And say: 'Truth has (now) arrived, and Falsehood perished: for Falsehood is (by its nature) bound to perish'. [17:78–81]

On the grave is a canopy inlaid with mother of pearl. It bears this chronogram:

[1] The sky on its four firm pillars repeated spontaneously the *takbir* four times [i.e., expressed wonder].

[2] He who turned his face away from this place turned his back on the great Ka'ba.

[3] And he who bowed the head to him made his face bright as a mirror.

[4] Should you serve as sweeper of his place [grave] you are capable of the work of a hundred messiahs.

[5] I searched for the date of this building, wisdom gave as inspiration, 'The dome of the Shaikh'.[237] [1017/1608–09]

Towards the top is inscribed in marble:

---

236 The *ayat Al-Kursi* (Quran, 2:255).

237 Zafar Hasan, Vol. II, p. 147. Zafar Hasan mentions the canopy as being made of wood, and adds an additional six verses before the ones noted by Sangin Beg.

[1]   He who becomes the slave of Nizam-ud-Din with his heart receives the royal
      crown of the whole world.

[2]   'Aziz-ud-Din [known as 'Alamgir II] performed the services of a slave with true
      faith: the kingly crown of Hind [India] has now been given me 'Aziz-ud-Din.

[3]   Through him is healed my wounded heart without recourse to food, prayer,
      medicine or physician.

[4]   Much afflicted are the people now, O beloved of God! [i.e., Nizam-ud-Din).
      Confer favour on sinners, you who are a friend of God.[238] [1169/1755–56]

Under the supervision of Hoshiar 'Ali Khan, the eunuch slave.

On the gates of the verandah towards the bottom, this inscription is engraved in marble:

> In the reign of his exalted Majesty Sahib Qiran-e-Sani [the second Lord of the
> happy conjunction i.e., Shah Jahan], the most humble of men Khalilullah Khan, son of
> Mir Miran Alhusaini Ni'matullahi, who was the governor of Shahjahanabad, erected
> this verandah round the blessed tomb in the year 1063 [1652–53].[239] The date of
> the death of Hazrat Nizam-ud-Din Auliya is eighteenth of Rabi'-us-Sani, 725 *Hijri*,
> Wednesday [3 April 1325].

Within the compound of the *dargah* of Hazrat Nizam-ud-Din Auliya, towards the foot of the grave, are two enclosures. In one enclosure are the graves of Emperor Muhammad Shah and his mother Nawab Qudsia Begam. On the headstone of the grave the *ayat Al-Kursi* is engraved. On the face of the headstone the *kalima* is written, and on the headstone of the grave of Muhammad Shah's mother, Qudsia Begam: 'O ye who believe! Bow down, prostrate yourselves, and adore your Lord; and do good; that ye may prosper. [22:77] Say: "O my Servants who"' till the *ayat* 'He is Oft-Forgiving, Most Merciful.' [39:53]

In the other enclosure is the grave of Jahan Ara, the daughter of Shah Jahan and a sister of 'Alamgir. On the headstone of the grave is inscribed:

---

238   Ibid., p. 148. This is one of the few inscriptions recorded that are in Urdu.

239   Zafar Hasan's quotation ends at this point. Ibid., p. 147.

He is living and self-subsisting.

[1] Let naught cover my grave save the green grass; for grass well suffices as a covering for the grave of the lowly.

The humble and mortal Jahan Ara, the disciple of the Khwajas of Chisht, and the daughter of Shah Jahan, the king and champion of faith, may God illuminate his demonstrations. [1092/1681][240]

In the second building is the dome of the grave of Amir Khusro. On a stone tablet in the enclosure [is written]:

There is no God but Allah, and Muhammad is His Messenger.

[1] The earth attained honour in the reign of Babur, the emperor and champion of the faith through the presence of this tablet.

[2] Mir Khusro the king of the kingdom of words [poetry], the ocean of accomplishment and sea of perfection;

[3] His prose is more attractive than flowing water, his poetry is clearer than pure water.

[4] [He is] a peerless singing nightingale and an incomparable sugar-tongued parrot.

[5] For the date of his death, when I bowed my head above the knees of thought,

[6] A chronogram gave 'Peerless' and another 'Sugar-tongued parrot'. [725 /1325]

[7] The tablet of my dust is without even a word of hope of a meeting with my beloved. My simplicity is the one sign of my true love.

Quatrain

[1] Mehdi Khwaja, a Sayyid of rank and dignity, became the founder of this matchless and incomparable building.

[2] I said, 'The good efforts of Mehdi Khwaja' when asked the date of the foundation of this building. [897/1491–92]

Written by Shihab, the enigmatist of Herat.[241]

---

[240] Ibid., p. 153.

[241] Ibid., p. 161. The several additions to the grave of Amir Khusro were made much after his death in 1325.

The inscriptions on the walls around the tomb, towards the east, are:

[1] O Khusro! Peerless in the world, I am a supplicant at thy tomb.

[2] It has been built by Tahir. An eternal blessing is always found here.

[3] Wisdom thus spake the date of its foundation, 'say to the tomb that it is a place of secrets'.

Towards the north:

> The composer of these lines, and founder of this building, is Tahir Muhammad 'Imad-ud-Din Hasan, son of Sultan 'Ali of Sabzwar, in the year 1014 *Hijri* [1605–06], may God forgive his sins and conceal his faults. The scribe 'Abd-un-Nabi, son of Ayyub.[242]

On the western face:

[1] O thou! Who hast the sweet drink of love in thy cup, and receivest messages constantly from the friend,

[2] In the journey through the two worlds, you arrive within the distance of your two steps.

[3] The house of Farid is ordered by thee, hence is it that thou art entitled Nizam.

[4] A hundred kind and pure souls, the sphere dissolves them, and your name forms them.

[5] The lot of those struck by the madness of love is relieved by the joy of your name.

[6] Your *dargah* is a Ka'ba for the angels. Their wings are like the pigeons on your roof.

[7] Immortal is the slave Khusro, for he with his thousand lives is thine own slave.[243]

Towards the south, a *mu'amma* [word puzzle] of the word 'Khusro':

---

[242] Ibid., p. 163.

[243] Ibid., p. 163. Zafar Hasan copied only three verses (numbers 1, 3 and 7); Sangin Beg's original has seven.

[1] My name is 'righteous' and 'Great Khwaja', it contains two *shins*, two *lams*, two *gafs* and two *jims*.

[2] If you can evolve my name from these letters I shall know that you are a wise man.

The scribe of the above is the grandson of Shaikh Farid Shakarganj.[244]

Towards the foot of the tomb of Amir Khusro is a triple doorway, within which is the grave of Mirdha Ikram. On the doorway of the enclosure is written:

[1] Ikram shone in the favour of the king as a particle of sand reflects the sun.

[2] He was buried at the feet of Khusro, and Sayyid said, 'Ikram attained rest at the feet of Khusro'.[245]

Towards the head of this grave, in a separate enclosure, are the headstones of two graves. On one of the headstones the *kalima-e-tayyib* is written, and under it the *ayat*:

Muhammad is the messenger of Allah; and those who are with him are strong against Unbelievers (till the end). [48:29] There is no God but He: That is the witness of Allah, His angels, and those endued with knowledge, standing firm on justice. There is no God but He, the Exalted in Power, the Wise. [3:18]

On the headstone's forehead: 'All that is on earth will perish:

But will abide (for ever) the Face of thy Lord, – full of Majesty, Bounty and Honour.' [55:26–27]

Under it the *kalima-e-tayyib* and all around the headstone the *ayat Al-Kursi* [are written]. On a tablet on the side is written:

---

244 Ibid., p. 163. A *mu'amma* is a word puzzle.

245 Ibid., p. 168. Zafar Hasan's copy of the inscription includes a date, 1216 *Hijri* [1801–02]. This is missing in Sangin Beg's manuscript, and Qasimi works out the chronogram to give 1226 *Hijri* [1811]. See Qasimi, p. 226.

Couplet

[1] O you without who, alas, the sphere turns without an axis! A thousand times alas, that the world is, but you are not!

Qit'a [couplet-sequence]

[1] Lamentations that in the end you left the assembly of life. The one because of whom all good and blessings were in this world.

[2] The *huma* [mythical bird] of the heavens, the Khwaja of the world. The heavens have never seen one like him, the grandest Khwaja.

[3] May he be blessed with witness and faith.

[4] All his nights passed in modesty and devotion; his days in repeating and reciting the Quran.

[5] Towards the garden of paradise, from the dwelling of the body, his pure soul made flight.

[6] From heaven, the *houris* gave his date: the Khwaja of the world, who has left it and come to this world. [770/1368]

On the second grave's headstone, which is the grave of the wife of Khwaja Jahan, the *ayat Al-Kursi* and the second *ayat* of the Holy Quran are engraved.

Outside the sandstone screen enclosure of the *dargah* of Hazrat Nizam-ud-Din, towards the east, is the tomb of Shams-ud-Din Muhammad Khan, husband of the foster mother of Emperor Akbar. During the reign of Akbar, Shams-ud-Din was killed at the entrance to Akbar's private apartments by a stab inflicted by Adham Khan with a dagger. The reason for this attack was that Adham Khan, who was the brother of Mirza Kokaltash Khan, titled Khan-e-A'zam, the son of Akbar's wet nurse Maham Anga, came with the evil intention of killing Emperor Akbar. Since Shams-ud-Din Muhammad Khan was always in attendance at the door, he stopped Adham Khan who was boldly entering the royal apartments and resisted him. Adham Khan killed him with a sword or dagger and entered the royal apartment in search of the emperor. As luck would have it the emperor himself decided to come out of his apartments at that very moment. He was either himself armed with a sword or an intimate gave him a sword. He saw that Adham Khan was advancing without check. The emperor challenged him in a tremendous voice and grabbing both hands of this villain with his hand, punched him so hard that he died. It is said that the emperor was twelve years old at the time.[246]

On the western gate of the tomb of Shams-ud-Din Muhammad Khan [is inscribed] the surat Al-Mulk till the ayat 'Did no Warner come to you?' [67:8] ('Inscribed by Baqi Muhammad'). Under this, at the threshold of the gate: 'He will provide'. On the mihrab of the north-facing gate: 'They will say, "Yes indeed; he did come"' [67:9] (up to the ayat) 'How terrible was my rejection of them!' [35:26] ('Inscribed by the nobody Baqi Muhammad Khan'). Under it [is written]:

> They rejoice in the bounty provided by Allah: And with regard to those left behind, who have not yet joined them (in their bliss), the (Martyrs) glory in the fact that on them is no fear, nor have they (cause to) grieve. [3:170]

Around the mihrab of the west-facing third door [is written]: 'Do they not observe the birds above them…?' [67:19] till 'I am (sent) only to warn plainly in public'. [67: 26] '(Inscribed by Baqi Muhammad)'. Under it, on the face of the threshold [is written]:

> And say not of those who are slain in the way of Allah: 'They are dead'. Nay, they are living, though ye perceive (it) not. [2:154]

Around the mihrab of the south-facing gate [is written]: 'At length, when they see it close at hand' till 'with clean-flowing water' [67:27–30], and the surat Al-Qadr till the end '(Inscribed by the katib Baqi Muhammad in 977 Hijri. This building was completed in 974 [1566–67])'.

Under the dome, on four sides, is inscribed in lapis lazuli:

[Masnavi 1]

Oh God, human life and lasting existence is through You.

---

[246] Shams-ud-Din Khan was the husband of Jiji Angah, Akbar's wet nurse, and Adham Khan was the son of the other wet nurse, Maham Anga. Sangin Beg's story is inaccurate in several details. In fact, Shams-ud-Din Khan was killed by Adham Khan and two others in an open courtyard. Akbar, emerging from his palace, did hit him, but Adham Khan died later, when he was thrown from the ramparts of the Agra fort. Akbar's age at the time was about twenty years. See Shireen Moosvi, Episodes in the Life of Akbar, National Book Trust, New Delhi, 1994, pp. 32–34.

Life and death are also in Your hands.
May You forever remain in this delightful world;
And in this field of day and night, may You always exist.

In this world, there are many others but none is like You:
You are an ocean of life, the rest is all a mirage.

I regard You as my place of safety and shelter,
In this world of trouble and war.

There is nothing except Your being, where we can seek solace.
That is why I look for Your favour and hope for Your benevolence upon me.

God, You are generous and kindness is Your quality.
All of Your creations look to You for favour.

Oh Lord, open the door to Your kindness and generosity to everyone;
And by forgiving them, grant them honour and success.

All my hope and fear are dependent on You,
For me it is You who are benevolent, who will grant us forgiveness.

Lord, gift us Your forgiveness.

[*Masnavi 2*]
Lord, all those who pay allegiance to your court.
Grace them all with such light which is hidden from us.
And grace us with that gift that is endless.
Through this pure Prophet, and on the Day of Judgement,
Bless and forgive Shams-ud-Din Muhammad's trespasses with your endless
benevolence.
And through the the light of the Prophet, show generosity to Yusuf Muhammad!

On the side of the headstone of the grave [is written:]

> Every soul shall have a taste of death: And only on the Day of Judgment shall you
> be paid your full recompense. Only he who is saved far from the Fire and admitted
> to the Garden . . . [3:185].

On both sides of the headstone [is written] the surat Al-Shams till 'Truly he succeeds that purifies it' [91:9]. On the headstone of his wife's grave the ayat Al-Kursi is written; and on its face: 'In the name of Allah, Most Gracious, Most Merciful. He is Allah and he dies not.' Outside the already mentioned dome is the grave of Khwajgi Darvesh. On a stone beside it is written:

> There is no God but Allah, and Muhammad is His Messenger.
> [1] Khwajgi Darwesh departed from this world and made heaven his abode;
> [2] He turned away from this mortal, temporal world,
> [3] And came to his Wali by right, with devotion.
> [4] Completely surrendering himself, he entered heaven and became free of this
>   existence.
> [5] Intelligence spoke his date thus: 'the dervish's life came to be uneternal'.
>   [990/1582–83] (Inscribed by 'Abd-us-Salam in 990 Hijri)

Towards the foot [of the grave is written]:

> O you without who, alas, the sphere turns without an axis! A thousand times alas,
> that the world is, but you are not!

Towards the top of the headstone [is written] 'All that is on earth will perish' [55:26], and on all four sides the ayat Al-Kursi is inscribed.

Ahead of this, near the kotla, Chaunsath Khamba is located. The number of its pillars is sixty-four. Its pillars, roof and walls are made of marble. In it is the grave of Mirza 'Aziz Kokaltash Khan, titled Khan-e-A'zam. Soon after Adham Khan died from the blow of the emperor – and some say he was poisoned by Maham Anga on the orders of the emperor – out of fear for his life Kokaltash became the spiritual disciple of the emperor and adopted his religion.[247] There are entrances all around this building.

On the western door [is written]: 'Allah, may he be praised and exalted, said, "Let not the Unbelievers think that"' till 'the bargain they made' [3:178–187]. On the northern entrance [is written]: 'They rejoice.' There is lattice work on the third and fourth doors.

On the headstone of the Great Khan's grave, in the Sulus script, in the *tughra* style, the *ayat Al-Kursi* is written.

Near the *kotla* of Hazrat Nizam-ud-Din Auliya, close to the wall, is the Kali Masjid, on the doorway of which this inscription is written:

> By the favour and grace of God, the most holy and omnipotent, in the reign of the king of the kings of the age, strong by the help of the Merciful, Abul Muzaffar Firoz Shah, the King, may God perpetuate his kingdom and increase his command and dignity, this mosque was built by the son of the slave of the threshold – which is as exalted in dignity as the heavens and is the sanctuary of the world – Junan Shah Maqbul, entitled Khan-e-Jahan, son of Khan-e-Jahan in the year 772 from the flight of the Prophet [1370–71], may God bless him and give him peace, and may God have compassion on that slave. Anyone offering praise in this mosque should remember this slave with a Fatiha and prayers for his faith.[248]

To the east of the said *kotla* of the shrine is the Arab Sarai. This is the property of Arabs and other general populace. On its eastern gateway is written:

> In the name of Allah, Most Gracious, Most Merciful. There is no God but Allah, and Muhammad is His messenger. Benevolence [*mihr*] the old mistress of Jahangir the King.[249]

---

[247] Here again Sangin Beg's account is doubtful. Mirza 'Aziz, Shams-ud-Din Khan's son, was a close companion of Akbar and much favoured, though he is said to have expressed some reservations about Akbar's religious predelictions.

[248] Zafar Hasan, Vol. II, p. 179.

[249] Ibid., p. 130. Slightly different versions are given in Zafar Hasan and Sangin Beg. The gate is believed to have been constructed by Mihr Banu, a eunuch.

Near the tomb of Emperor Humayun and adjoining the wall of the Arab Sarai is a mosque. This chronogram is inscribed on it:

> This was written in the reign of [after several titles] Jalal-ud-Din Muhammad Akbar Shah Badshah.
>
> [1]   Nawab Begam, who is valued even by the sky, and was a benefactress of the world like the divine shadow;
>
> [2]   In Delhi she constructed many mosques, *khanqahs* and *sarais* for divine recompense.
>
> [3]   From all this was built this Masjid-e-Jami', which is heart-delighting like the palace of heaven.
>
> [4]   This work was completed under the arrangement of the Khwaja.
>
> [5]   When I asked its date, intelligence replied: 'This place was built for worship.'
>
> [986/1578–79][250]

Close to it is the tomb of Emperor Humayun. The date of his death is derived from this hemistich: 'The emperor Humayun fell from the roof' [962/1554–55]. Humayun was buried within the limits of Old Dehli near the *dargah* of the Mahbub-e-Ilahi [Nizam-ud-Din Auliya]. His age was forty-nine years, four months and two days. Similarly, the duration of his reign according to lunar calculations was twenty-five years, two months and five days. Of this twenty-five-year period of his reign, Humayun was Emperor of Hindustan for nineteen years the first time, and the second time he reigned for approximately two years and two months. In the fourth year of the reign of Emperor Akbar, the foundation stone of the tomb of Emperor Humayun 'Jannat Ashiyani' was laid. The tomb was completed after sixteen years, at an expense of fifteen lakh rupees.[251] Emperor Akbar was born of Hamida Bano in Amarkot. Hamida Bano was of the family of Ahmad Jaam.

The list of emperors and others buried in Humayun's tomb:

The graves of Emperor Humayun and Mariam Makani; the grave of Haji Begam,

---

[250]   Qasimi, p. 232. This may be the building that is popularly referred to as the Afsarwala Mosque. Zafar Hasan, Vol. II, pp. 132–33.

[251]   Sangin Beg's dates are quite confused as to Humayun's reign as well as for the construction of the tomb. Humayun reigned during 1530–40 and 1555–56. The tomb was built between 1565 and 1572.

Humayun's wife; the grave of Faridun, Humayun's grandson; the grave of Hafiz-un-Nisa; Bilal Khwaja Sara; the grave of Humayun's concubines, Sadr-un-Nisa, Manija Khanam and Fataha Khanam; Prince Hakim Muhammad; Prince 'Ali Hakim; Khurshid Bakht, the brother of Muhammad Akbar Shah Mouz-ud-Din, the grandfather of Shah 'Alam; the grave of 'Alamgir II; Princess Ladli Begam; Mubarak Shah, the son of 'Alamgir II; Farrukh Shah, the son of Emperor 'Alamgir; Dara Shukoh and Sulaiman Shukoh, the brothers of Aurangzeb; Emperor Farrukh Shah, Kam Bakhsh, the brother of 'Alamgir II; Mirza Farkhanda Bakht, the son of Shah 'Alam; Jani Begam, the daughter of Mirza Farkhanda Bakht; Mirza Firoz Bakht, the son of Shah 'Alam; Nawab Shah Abadi, the mother of Firoz Bakht; Sangi Begam, the daughter of Aurangzeb; and the grave of Bahadur Shah, the son of Mirza Jahangir Bahadur.

The following is inscribed on the grave of Bahadur Shah:

[1]   Bahadur Shah travelled from this world suddenly, alas!

[2]   The angels spoke of his year: 'The brave one who got a place in heaven.'

[1229/1813–14]

Within the compound of Humayun's tomb is located a dome. In it are two graves. Outside the compound of the tomb, towards the east, is a blue dome which is known as Maqbara Hajjam.[252] There is, however, no trace of a grave in it. It is broken down and has become anonymous. Close to Humayun's tomb, towards the Purana Qil'a, is 'Azim Ganj, which is now deserted. Behind the settlement of the Kotla Nizam-ud-Din Auliya and the Arab ki Sarai constructed by Mihr Banu is a rainwater canal.[253] This side of the canal is the grave of Sayyid Nur Muhammad Badayuni. This man was a noble and a godly elder. Near the Arab Sarai are wells of sweet water. Also close to the Arab Sarai is the tomb of the son of Nawab Bairam Khan, 'Abdur Rahim Khan-e-Khanan,[254] who was among the big nobles of Emperor Jahangir's reign. There is a famous Hindi saying connected with Khan-e-Khanan: 'Khan-e-Khanan, *tere khane mein batana*'

---

[252]   Today the former dome is called Maqbara-e-Hajjam or barber's tomb, and the latter, Neela Gumbad.

[253]   No doubt the stream known today as Barahpullah.

[254]   Bairam Khan, a trusted and very high-ranking noble of Humayun's reign who held the empire together after the latter's death. His son 'Abdur Rahim inherited his father's title of Khan-e-Khanan ('lord of lords'), and is today best known for his Hindi poetry. He died in 1627.

(Khan-e-Khanan, a jewel in your food), which alludes to the fact that the said Khan was very generous. Whoever he gave food to, he would first put gold or silver in the dish, fill it with food and then give it to the poor, the needy, religious mendicants and beggars.

At a distance of 1 *kos* from here is a bridge which is known as Barahpula. It has eleven arched openings. This is engraved on red stone on the bridge:

Allah is great.

[1]   Jahangir Shah, the son of Akbar Shah, whose light of justice is established in the world.

[2]   To friends he is the hoopoe, to enemies the tumult of the ring-dove.

[3]   During his sultanate, India was referred to as Istanbul.

[4]   The revered Dehli is a garden which took colour and perfume from the flowers.

[5]   In the seventh year of his sultanate, the nightingale is crying due to the flower's cruelty.

[6]   His most devoted and affectionate servant, Agha, the chief servant of the palace, a confidante of the king,

[7]   He constructed this bridge with great indulgence that it became a landmark for all.

[8]   From the sky I asked the year of its making, its face bloomed like the sun,

[9]   It said, 'Pick up the pen and write, "the bridge was his deed of kindness."'

[1021/1612–13]

In the neighbourhood of this bridge are a few *pakka sarais*. One of them is known as Chhoti Sarai. Besides this is Sarai Qalaj Khan, which is known as Qala' Khan.[255] At a distance of 1 *kos* from here, within the limits of the *mauza*-e-Kilokhari, is the grave

---

255 Now called Sarai Kale Khan and the site of a major bus terminus.

of Sayyid Mahmud Bahar. Here lies the grave of Shaikh Rukn-ud-Din Firdausi.[256] Khizrabad and the *sarai* of Mahtab Khan are located near it. Gujars live in this *sarai*. After this is Sarai Julena. Near this is the lake of Kishan Das. After this is *mauza-e-*Badarpur and a canal.

After this is a *sarai* known as Khwaja ki Sarai. And then a bridge which is known by the name of Pul-e-Sirsa. After this is *mauza-e-*Faridabad, which was founded by Shaikh Farid, the son of the teacher of Emperor Jahangir. Faridabad is at a distance of 12 *kos* from the *Dar-ul-Khilafa* of Dehli.

From the settlement of Jai Singhpura to the *dargah* of Khwaja Qutb-ud-Din

First there is Jai Singhpura, a police *chowki*, and a *baoli* close to the Hanuman Mandir, a three-bay *dalan*, [and] the garden of Guruji Pandit where there is a stall dispensing free drinking water. Close to this is a settlement of the ice-makers. Close to the wells, towards the settlement of the ice-makers, is *mauza-e-*Raisina. This land has been bought by Nawab Mirza Mahmud Khan Bahadur. At the wells here, charitable water stalls are set up during 'Ashura in Muharram.[257] At the white well, otherwise known as Dhaula Kuan, are the mosque, *baoli* and garden of Muhammad Khan Karora. Behind this to the south, towards the city, is the garden of Nabi Bakhsh Khan, who was the son of Miyan Khan, brother of Maroha Ikram. After this is the tomb of the late Safdar Jang, who was the minister of Emperor Ahmad Shah and died on 18 Zil-Hajj. This tomb was built at a cost of three lakhs of rupees under the supervision of Shidi Hilal Muhammad Khan. Close to this tomb are three domed buildings. One of these is the tomb of Emperor Mubarak Shah, who was a descendant of the Prophet through his daughter Fatima. The other domed buildings are of the Afghan *sardars* of this period.[258] Here there is the *mauza-e-*Jorbagh. Towards the city is the *mauza-e-*Chhatarpur where the Gujars live. Here, too, there are tombs and mosques built by earlier emperors. From here to the

---

[256] These two graves are in Kilokri village. Mahmood Bahar and Rukn-ud-Din were both contemporaries of Nizam-ud-Din Auliya.

[257] The tenth day of the month of Muharram. The water-stalls were no doubt for the processions of mourning commemorating the tragedy of Karbala.

[258] This is now the Lodi Garden.

Dehli Gate of the city is, firstly, Sarban [camel driver] Sarai, and, then, Zabita Ganj.[259]

To the south of *mauza*-e-Jorbagh is Karbala, which was built by Mirza Ashraf Beg Khan. Here the *tazias* of the city are buried on the day of 'Ashura in Muharram.[260] After this is the *mauza* of 'Ali Ganj, i.e. the compound of the *dargah* of 'Ali Shah Mardan.[261] On its northern gate is this inscription in Nasta'liq script:

> Muhammad the friend of God said, 'I am a city of learning and 'Ali is its gateway.' In the auspicious reign of Ahmad Shah Bahadur, the king and champion of faith, the building of the fort, the Majlis Khana [the congregation house], the mosque and the tank, was completed in one year, according to the orders of Her Highness Nawab Qudsia Sahiba Zamaniya, under the supervision of Nawab Bahadur Javed Khan Sahib, and under the control of the humble Lutf 'Ali Khan. 1163 [1750–51].[262]

In the *dargah*, at the northern corner of the marble tank near the footprint of Hazrat 'Ali, is the following inscription:

> On the piece of ground where there is a mark of your foot, for years there will be prostrations by men of insight. [1173/1759–60]. Allah Muhammad 'Ali.[263]

Inside the *dargah*, towards the Majlis Khana of the late Nazir Ishrat 'Ali Khan, the Muhalli (eunuch steward of the harem) of Huzur-e-Wala Muhammad Akbar Shah Badshah-e-Ghazi, on the northern gate of the western wall, the following inscription is written:

[1] At the court of the emperor of both the worlds, 'Ali, the king of heroes and the friend of God,

[2] By order of the renowned king Akbar, when Ishrat 'Ali Khan adorned the place,

---

259 This is where Rajpath is located, on the greens of which the Zabita Ganj mosque still stands. Zabita Khan was an important nobleman during the first half of the reign of Shah 'Alam II.

260 This practice is still followed.

261 The shrine houses a footprint of 'Ali, the son-in-law of the Prophet.

262 Zafar Hasan, Vol. II, p. 195.

263 Ibid., p. 200.

[3] I enquired of the Sayyid the year of its foundation, and he wrote, 'Nazir built it'. 1223 *Hijri* [1808–09][264]

In front of the *dargah* is the grave of Nawab Musa Khan, which has the following inscription at its head:

> In the name of Allah, Most Gracious, Most Merciful.
> O Veiler of faults. O Forgiveness. O Benevolence. O Benign One. O Rizwan.
> O Pardoner of sins, He is the Ever-Living One Who never dies.
> [1] The lamp of the chamber of the seventh Imam slept at the foot of 'Ali, the king of heroes.
> [2] When I asked the invisible crier the date [of his death], he said, 'Iram is the dwelling of Muswi Khan'. [1184/1770–71][265]

Here there are also the graves of the daughter of Shah 'Alam, her daughter Nawasi Begam and other princes. There is the grave of Shah Arif 'Ali Sahib, a three-arched gateway, a *naqqar khana* built by Sadiq 'Ali Khan, the house of Mirza Ashraf Beg Khan, the *haveli* built by Zinat *tawaif*, a *baoli*, mosque gate and other buildings. There are also the *havelis* of the *khadims* of the *dargah* and others, and the property of the Gujars.

Adjoining the eastern gateway of the *kotla* of the *dargah* is the tomb and garden of Nawab Mubarak Mahal Begam Sahiba, the mother of Muhammad Akbar Shah Ghazi. Outside the southern gate of the *kotla* of the *dargah* is the tomb of the deceased Nawab Najaf Khan Bahadur. This chronogram is inscribed on the grave:

> He is the Pardoner.
> In the name of Allah, Most Gracious, Most Merciful.
> [1] This sky of crooked nature, with its back [bent] like a bow, and full of arrows, which with the arrow of misfortune does not miss the mark,
> [2] Shot at the most noble of Sayyids, through whom there was honour to the lineage of Safavi Sayyids.

---

[264] Ibid., p. 201.

[265] Ibid., p. 206. For Najaf Khan, see note 88 above.

[3] [Who was] a worthy fruit of the tree of the garden of eight and four [i.e. the twelve Imams of the Shi'as], a pure splendour of two pearls [Hasan and Husain], and a gem of nine shells [skies].

[4] [Named] Bakhshi-ul-Mulk Amir Najaf Khan, the lion-hearted and the conqueror of countries of India with the help of [the command] 'Be not afraid'.

[5] A hero, if he held Zulfiqar [the name of the two edged sword of 'Ali] in his hand, the king would exclaim, 'a worthy son'.

[6] May he be a companion of the last of the Prophets [Muhammad] with his ancestor, the revealer of the secrets 'if it can be revealed'.

[7] The pen of 'Ali, which is a twin brother of the Divine revelation, wrote the date of his death on his ashes [grave], 'This is the grave of Najaf'.[266]

[1196/1781–82]

On the side of the grave of Afrasiyab, which lies to the south of the grave of the late Nawab, is this writing:

He is the Pardoner.

In the name of Allah, Most Gracious, Most Merciful.

[1] *Bakhshi* of the realm Ashraf-ud-Daulah alias Afrasiyab, rests near Najaf Khan, at the door of the king of Najaf.

[2] If one looks at the ornament of the honour of his witness, it says, 'the date of the Sayyid is he who is resurrected with the king of witnesses'. [1198–99/1784]

1199 *Hijri*, seventeenth of the month of Zil-Hajj, Tuesday, the twenty-sixth regnal year of Shah 'Alam Badshah-e-Ghazi. May Allah throw light on His Proof.

To the east of this is *mauza*-e-Kotla.[267] Here is the tomb of the Ghori emperors. At a distance of less than half a *kos* from here is the Masjid Moth,[268] which was built during the reign of Shah Jahan. The mosque had a courtyard which has now fallen down from the top, but its walls remain. The *surat Al-Mulk* till 'unto Him is the Resurrection' is

---

[266] Zafar Hasan, Vol. II, p. 211.

[267] Kotla Mubarakpur, which has the tomb of the Syed ruler Mubarak Shah (r. 1433–45).

[268] This beautiful mosque was actually built in 1505 by Miyan Bhoiya, minister of Emperor Sikandar Lodi.

engraved over its entrance. Inside the mosque, the *ayat Al-Kursi* is inscribed above the high *mihrab*. Under this, the *surah*: 'Whatever is in the heavens and on earth, doth declare the Praises and Glory of Allah, – the Sovereign, the Holy One' till 'people who do wrong' [62:1–5] [is written]. Under it the *kalima-e-shahadat*: 'I bear witness that there is no God except Allah; One is He, no partner hath He, and I bear witness that Muhammad is His Servant and Messenger.' Under the same *mihrab* [are written] the *kalima-e-tayyib, sur ul Al-Ikhlas* and *surat Al-Falaq* The *kalima-e-tayyib* is engraved in a circular pattern on both sides of the above-mentioned entrance.

At a distance of one-and-a-half *kos* from here is the *dargah* of Hazrat Nasir-ud-Din Chiragh-e-Dehli. Here it is engraved in marble:

> In the name of Allah, Most Gracious, Most Merciful.
> The dome of this building was built in the times of [after several titles] Firoz Shah [followed by titles]. This work was finished in 772 *Hijri*.

The following is written in golden lettering inside the dome, on the western wall, of the tomb of Hazrat Nasir-ud-Din:

> Muhammad   Allah   Allah   Muhammad

It is said about the death of Khwaja Nasir-ud-Din that he died on the eighteenth of the holy month of Ramzan 757 *Hijri* [1356] and was buried in Old Dehli. In the mosque of this *dargah* there is a bed which is made of a single piece of wood with no joints. The width of this bed is one-and-a-half yards, its length three yards, and its height ten yards. On a short side of the bed is inscribed:

> This wooden bed is an offering of Dakhni Beg to his holiness Nasir-ud-Din Mahmud Chiragh-e-Dehli, may God purify his cherished secrets. The year 1142 *Hijri* [1729–30] corresponding to the twelfth year of the reign of Muhammad Shah.[269]

Behind the mosque here lies the tomb of Emperor Bahlol, the son of Sultan

---

269 Zafar Hasan, Vol. III, p. 133.

Sikandar.[270] Near the compound of the *dargah* of Hazrat Chiragh-e-Dehli is the tomb of Shaikh Salah Feil Safed. The date of his death is 22 Jamadi-us-Sani 753 *Hijri* [1352]. Near this is the grave of Shaikh Shah 'Abdullah Qureshi who died on 22 Safar 894 *Hijri* [1489].

At a distance of one-and-a-half *kos* from Chiragh-e-Dehli is the temple of Kalkaji, a place of worship for the Hindus. At a distance of two-and-a-half *kos* from here is Tughlaqabad. The details of Tughlaq that are related are as follows. His name was Ghazi Malik bin Tughlaq. He was from among the old nobles of Sultan Qutb-ud-Din Mubarak Shah and 'Ala-ud-Din Khilji. He had been deputed to Multan to stop the advance of the Mongols. After the departure of the Mongols, his son Malik Fakhr-ud-Din Jona, titled 'Sultan Muhammad Tughlaq Shah', came accompanied by the ruler of Bahram and Dipalpur to avenge the murder of his benefactor Sultan Qutb-ud-Din Mubarak Shah.[271] Near Dehli he engaged in battle with the murderer of his benefactor, the impudent and disloyal Khusro Khan. Having gained victory over this ingrate he came into the palace at Siri, and gathered together the high and mighty, the notables, the learned, the scholarly, the judges, the descendants of the Prophet, the saints and the people of the city. These people wept bitterly at the murder of their benefactor, and his sons Manku Khan and Anku Khan. Ghazi Malik told all those present, 'I have avenged the murder of my benefactor by Khusro Khan and have murdered him. Now whatever descendants of the 'Alai and Qutbi families are

---

[270] Bahlol Lodi, the founder of the Lodi dynasty, reigned during 1451–88. Not all historians are convinced that this is the tomb of Bahlol Lodi. It has been argued that his tomb might be the one in the Lodi Garden known as Sheesh Gumbad. See Simon Digby, 'The tomb of Buhlūl Lōdī', *Bulletin of the School of Oriental and African Studies*, 38, 1975, pp. 550–61.

[271] The last Khilji ruler (r. 1316–20).

present may be brought here and seated on the throne of the sultanate.' All said, 'you have avenged us Muslims on this ingrate Khusro Khan and his cruel brother and have delivered us from their grasp. You are therefore worthy of the sultanate and have the right to be emperor.' Thus, with the consent of everybody, Ghazi Malik was taken by the hand and seated on the throne. He had prostrated himself at this very throne for ages. He was given the title Sultan Ghiyas-ud-Din Tughlaq Shah. Only Allah is wise.

This emperor's tomb is near the Tughlaqabad fort. There are three graves here. One belongs to Tughlaq Shah, another to Tughlaq Shah's son Sultan 'Adil, and the third is the grave of Tughlaq Shah's wife. Within the doorway of the tomb is a *dalan*. This has four doors and one pillar. It has twenty-two steps. There is a bridge between the fort and the tomb. Within the fort is the mosque of Shaikh Farid,[272] the *bakhshi* of Emperor Jahangir. He had founded Faridabad. This mosque bears the following inscription:

> Allah is great. In the days of Jahangir Badshah [his several titles], the younger Master Shaikh Farid, who was also known as Murtaza Khan Bukhari, laid the foundations of this mosque. Shaikh 'Abdullah Ansari finished the construction on 2 Rajab, 1027 *Hijri* [1618]. It was constructed in honour of Amin-ud-Daulah.

This fort has seven foundations, 56 gates, 52 *chowks* and one *baoli*.[273]

At a distance of half a *kos* to the south of the settlement of Chiragh-e-Dehli is the Kali Masjid. This mosque was also built by Khan-e-Jahan. It is said that before this mosque was built, there was a *mauza* here which was known by the name of *mauza-e-Khidki*. These days this mosque is called Masjid-e-Khidki. Gujars and Jats live in this mosque. This mosque has 99 domes and four *chowks*. There are seven such mosques as have been built by Khan Jahan. His grave is in the mosque of the *Dar-ul-Khilafa*. The list of the seven mosques is as follows.

The first is the Kali Masjid, which is located in the area of Turkman Gate in Shahjahanabad. The second is located at the fourway intersection of Qadam Sharif. The third is close to the Kotla Firoz Shah. The fourth is in the Kotla of Hazrat Nizam-ud-Din Auliya. The fifth is in *mauza*-e-Kalu Sarai near Chiragh-e-Dehli. The sixth is near the *dargah* of Bibi Nur and is famous as the Masjid-e-Begampur. The seventh is known as Khidki Masjid.[274]

A grave is located near the Khidki *mauza*. On it is engraved:

---

272 Shaikh Farid Bukhari is said to have died in 1616, in which case the construction of the mosque was finished after his death.

273 This large fort has more than one *baoli*.

274 Not all agree with this list. The Begampur Masjid is believed to have been built during the reign of Muhammad Shah Tughlaq.

[1] My heart-stealer with playful eyes, 'in Allah's name'. The suffering has arrived in my life, 'in Allah's name'.

[2] For murdering the poor hapless one, the sword of the eyebrow is drawn, 'in Allah's name'.

Near the Masjid-e-Begampur is the grave of Shaikh Farid, which has this inscription:

Praise be to Allah who liveth and dieth not.

In the time of his late majesty Jalal-ud-Din Akbar, the king and champion of the faith, Farid-ud-Din Sayyid Ahmad Bukhari was honoured with his majesty's favour, and during the just reign of Nur-ud-Din Jahangir, the king, he was distinguished with the title of Murtaza Khan. He died in the ninth year of [Jahangir's] accession corresponding to 1025 *Hijri* [1616–17].

[1] When Murtaza Khan died, he made a conquest of the eternal world.

[2] The angels said for the chronogram, 'O God! May his soul be illuminated!'[275]

In the area of *mauza*-e-Khidki, the tomb of Yusuf Qattal is located. At the top of the headstone of this grave is written: 'There is no God but Allah, and Muhammad is His Messenger'. Towards the middle, on both sides, is written: 'Allah'. At the top of the base is engraved:

The construction of this domed building was in the time of Sikandar Shah [several titles mentioned], and was constructed by 'Ala-ud-Din Nur Taj who is a grandson of Shaikh Farid Shakar Ganj. The month of Muharram, the year 903 [1497].

After this, on the road that leads to the *dargah* of Khwaja Qutb-ud-Din, near the *dargah* of Bibi Nur, to the east, is an enclosed garden.[276] Within this is a *pakka chabutra* [bricked platform]. On its wall is this inscription:

O Allah! O Muhammad! In the name of God who is merciful and compassionate, and

---

275 Zafar Hasan, Vol. III, p. 153.

276 The remains of this are in Adhchini village.

the last of the prophets; may [divine] blessings be upon him! At the place where I secured the blessed hand-impression of His Holiness [the Prophet], I heard that in the honoured Mecca on the mount Hira, which is also called Jabali Saur [sic], there is an impression of the luminous body of His Holiness on a stone, whereon at the commencement of the *wahi* [the divine revelation], Gabriel, peace be upon him, cut open the enlightened bosom and filled it with [divine] light. And in the cave of Jabali Saur [sic], wherein His Holiness had concealed himself at the time of flight, there is an impression of the side and the back of the sacred hand, and impressions of the feet of a doe and of her fawn as well as the marks of drops of her milk. And [once] His Holiness was going to Masjid-ul-Haram to say his prayers when someone in Zuqaqul Hajar said regretfully that the congregational prayer was over. His Holiness reclined against the wall whereupon the blessed elbow penetrated into the stone. From the wall on the left side a stone said, 'The congregation is ready', and that liar was Satan. The mark of the tongue of the stone is visible. At the end of *Kitabul Ilam bi Alami Baitul Haram* the places of pilgrimage are noticed, and an extract of the notice is: between the house of the Prophet and that of Her Holiness Khadija there is a mosque on the road, in the street named Zuqaqul Mirfaq. At that place there was a house together with a shop of Siddiq Akbar where he sold wool, and near it on the wall there is a stone containing the mark of an elbow. It is written in *Bahrul Amiq* quoted from *Zubdatul Amal* that the mark is of the elbow of the blessed arm. And Taqi Qudsi in the *History of Mecca* says, 'People visit it and say that His Holiness reclined against the stone and talked with another stone which was before him to the left. They visit it also.' Probably this stone is the same about which His Holiness said, 'I know a stone in Mecca which, whenever I passed it, saluted me.' And on the mount Abu Qubais there are the tombs of their Holiness Adam, Eve and Shis – may peace be upon them. An extract from the notice in the *Tarikh-e-Aziri* [sic] is that in obedience to Gabriel, His Holiness Abraham, may peace be upon both of them, laid the boundaries of the *haram* [sanctuary] of the blessed Mecca with mud and stone, and boundary towards 'Arafat is the mount Namira, eleven *kiroh* from Mecca. At the foot of the mountain, in a cave, there is a place to which His Holiness repaired daily. In the early days the angels brought down a tent of red ruby with three chandeliers of gold and the *Hajrul Aswad* [sic] from Adam from paradise in the light of stars, and marked a site for the Ka'ba. Their light reached as far as the boundaries of the *haram* and angels standing on those boundaries guarded the tent so that the devils should not see it. And Gabriel left Adam, may peace be upon him, at Mina and asked his desires. Adam said, 'I ask for paradise' and for this reason it was called Mina. At 'Arafat there was performed the miracle of *shaqq-ul-qamar* [splitting of the moon]. At a sign from the blessed finger [the moon] was rent into two halves, and it is proved from the Quran and Hadith that each of the two halves parting from each other was raised to heaven. This was caused to be written by Muhammad Ma'sum entitled I'tibar Khan 'Azim-ush-Shani [*sic*]. The fourth year of the august [reign] of Muhammad Farrukhsiyar, the victorious king. The year 1127.[277]

Adjoining the wall of this garden, beside the road, is a well. There is something written inside it. Near it, beside the road, to the south, is the *dargah* of Bibi Nur. Here there is the grave of the honourable mother of Hazrat Nizam-ud-Din Auliya.[278] Behind this is a tomb which is known as 'Uncha Maqbara'. The *mauza-e-Hauz Khas* is here.[279] Firoz Shah's tomb is here. Above the entrance of this tomb, whatever words are legible, they are being copied here and those letters which have dropped off are not presented here. First of all, the *kalima-e-tayyib*:

> There is no God but Allah, and Muhammad is His Messenger.
> Constructed by the Sultan of Sultans Firoz Shah [followed by titles]

The second line:

> He ordered … of Sultans, Sultan Sikandar, son of the Sultan of Sultans Sultan Bahlol Shah [his titles] in the holy month of Ramzan, in the year 930 … of Sultans, Sultan Firoz Shah, may he rest in peace and may heaven be his abode.

There are eight *mihrabs* under the dome, above which is written, on the first *mihrab*: 'In the name of Allah, Most Gracious, Most Merciful. The first House of

---

[277] Zafar Hasan, Vol. III, pp. 198–99. The date converts to 1715–16.

[278] The *dargah* known as Mai Sahiba is also in Adhchini.

[279] In fact, Hauz Khas is at quite a distance north from Adhchini.

worship appointed for men was that at Bakka: Full of blessing' till the *ayat* 'Pilgrimage thereto is a duty men owe to Allah' [3:96–97]. On the second *mihrab*: 'In the name of Allah, Most Gracious, Most Merciful. Had We sent down this Quran' till 'that they may reflect'. [59:21] Above the third *mihrab*: 'Allah is He' till 'the Irresistible, the Supreme' [59:23]. Above the fourth *mihrab*: 'Glory to Allah! (High is He) above the partners they attribute to Him. He is Allah, the Creator, the Evolver, the Bestower of Forms' till 'He is the Exalted in Might, the Wise'. [59:24] Above the fifth *mihrab*: the *ayat Al-Kursi* till 'as He permitteth'. On the sixth *mihrab*: [continued from the *ayat Al-Kursi*] 'He knoweth what appeareth to His creatures as before' till 'He is the Most High, the Supreme'. Above the seventh *mihrab*: 'Say: O Allah! Lord of Power' till 'over all things Thou hast power'. [3:26] Above the eighth *mihrab*: 'Thou causest the night to gain on the day' till 'without measure'. [3:27]

On all sides of the dome, Allah's 99 names are written in the Sulus script. On the dome's ceiling, the complete *ayat Al-Kursi* and, in circles, the *kalima-e-tayyib* are written. The year of Firoz Shah's death is 790 *Hijri* [1388–89]. The root of the chronogram is 'the death of Firoz'. Here are the remains of a grave near the tomb

of Firoz Shah. It is said that this is the grave of the Badshah-e-Rum and has been in existence since before the reign of Firoz Shah.[280] Only Allah is wise.

There is a tomb near Hauz Khas. It has an inscription in blue stone on the outside, on the western wall, engraved in the Sulus script:

> The foundation of this building was laid in the time of Sultan Muhammad Shah [several titles mentioned].... This blue dome was constructed by Shaikh Shihab-ud-Din Taj Khan and Sikandar Shah Sultan Abu Sa'id on 9 Ramzan, 906 *Hijri*. [1501–02]

Inside the tomb are written the 99 names of God, the verse *Al-Kursi* and, on the western wall, 'Allah' in the outline of a *surahi*.[281] There is a well near this tomb which has an inscription inside it that is illegible. At a distance of 1 *kos* from Hauz Khas, to the south, are the tombs of Mir Khan and Wazir Khan. It is said that they were companions of Firoz Shah. One of these is known as *mauza*-e-Mirpur and the other, *mauza*-e-Wazirpur. There is another tomb here known as Muhammadpur.[282] It has not been possible to find out the date of its construction or its correct name. There is nothing written on it.

Masjid Quwwat-ul-Islam

There is a tower here by the name of Khwaja Sahab ki Lath. The foundation of this mosque was laid by the order of Sultan Shihab-ud-Din alias Mouz-ud-Din in 606 *Hijri* [1209–10]. Sultan Shams-ud-Din Altamash took the responsibility of completing it with his own hands. During his lifetime he left no stone unturned in the completion of this mosque and tower. The said mosque is located near the *dargah* of Khwaja Qutb-ud-Din Bakhtiyar Kaki. On the eastern side of its enclosure is an inscription: 'The foundation of this mosque was laid by Qutb-ud-Din [followed by titles and prayer]'. Above the northern entrance, which Sultan Shihab-ud-Din constructed, the following is engraved:

---

[280] It is not known which grave is being referred to here. Rum refers to Turkey.

[281] Qasimi, pp. 246–47. The tomb is known as Bagh-e-'Alam ka Gumbad.

[282] This tomb is known as Muhammadpur Tin Burji, and around it is the village of Muhammadpur.

In the name of Allah, Most Gracious, Most Merciful.

But Allah doth call to the Home of Peace: He doth guide whom He pleaseth to a way that is straight. [10:25]

This great building was ordered by the sublime Sultan [followed by titles] Muhammad Bin Saam in the year 592.[283] [1195–96]

This mosque had eleven arched entrances, of which the remains of ten are still visible, but most have broken down over the arch. Above the first entrance [is written] [the surat] Al-Mulk from the beginning till 'the Resurrection' [ayat 15]. Towards its side is a mihrab. Above it are written the surat Al-Ikhlas and the kalima-e-tayyib. Below this is written the ayat Al-Kursi. Above the second entrance, the surah 'Verily We have granted thee a manifest Victory' till 'a goodly reward' is written. [48:1–16] Above the middle mihrab the ayat 'In order that ye may believe in Allah' till 'morning and evening' [48:9] [is written]. Below this [is written]: 'There is no God but He: That is the witness of Allah' till 'He, the Exalted in Power, the Wise'. [3:18] Above the third entrance [is written] the surah 'Most Gracious' till 'not without authority shall ye be able to pass! Then which of the favours of your Lord will ye deny?' [55:1–34] Above the fourth entrance, which lies in the enclosure, the surat [Al] 'Imran [is written] till 'never fails in His promise'. [3:1–9] Above the fifth entrance, the surat Al-Furqan [is written] till 'between those extremes'. [25:1–67] The sixth doorway is at the centre and is bigger than all the others. Around its mihrab the surah 'The believers must eventually win through' is written till the ayat 'on the Day of Judgment, will ye be raised up'. [23:1–16] Below this, in the second circle, something is written in the Kufic script, but due to its antiquity it has broken down in several places and become indecipherable. After this in the third circle [is written:] 'Glory to Allah Who did take His servant for a Journey' till the ayat 'the more numerous in man-power'. [17:1–6] At this place, the date [of construction] of this mosque is written [in Arabic]: 'five hundred and ninety-four' [1197–98]. Above the seventh entrance, the surat 'Verily We have granted thee a Victory' till 'the highest achievement' [is written] [48:1–5]. Above the eighth entrance [is written]: 'A.L.M. Allah! There is no God but He, the Living, the Self-Subsisting, Eternal. It is He Who sent down to thee the Book' till 'a

---

[283] Zafar Hasan gives the date for the construction of the mosque as 1191, and for the minar, the early thirteenth century.

warning for such as have eyes to see.' [3:1–13] Above the ninth entrance [is written:] 'Be quick in the race for forgiveness from your Lord' till 'the best of helpers.' [3:133–50] The tenth and eleventh entrances do not have any writing left because of being in ruins.

In the courtyard of the mosque there is a pillar of iron. Though it is popularly connected with Rai Pithora, this is not correct. Because there were no clocks in this period, it was built to determine the time of day. The clock was invented during the reign of Firoz Shah, and became popular throughout the world.

Description of the tower of this mosque, which the common people call Khwaja Qutb-ud-Din ki Lath

Sultan Shams-ud-Din Altamash had it built. 'Altamash' refers to the fact that due to being born at a time of the eclipse of the sun or the moon, his little finger and the finger next to it were joined together. He was therefore called Altamash. This is a Turki word. On the door to the tower is written:

> The Messenger of Allah, may Allah bless him and bring peace on him, said, 'he who constructs a mosque, Allah will construct a house like it for him in paradise.'
> The blessed building of the tower is the servitude of the honourable Sultan of Sultans, the sun of the world and the faith, may he receive mercy and forgiveness, may he rest in peace and be granted a place in heaven (the writing has broken down from this point).
> This tower was repaired on the first of Rabi'-ul-Akhir 909 [23 September 1503] under the supervison of Fateh Khan, son of Khawas Khan, during the reign of Sikandar Shah [several titles mentioned], son of Bahlol Shah [followed by posthumous titles].[284]

Over the doorway at the top of the tower is written:

> This *minar* was injured by lightning in the year 770 [1368–69]. By the divine grace, Firoz Sultan, who is exalted by the favour of the most Holy, built this portion of

---

[284] Qasimi, p. 250.

the edifice with care. May the inscrutable Creator preserve it from all calamities.[285]

Above this, on a slab of marble, the following is written covering all the sides:

> ⸫ This building was ordered in the days of the realm of the great Sultan, the sublime
> king of kings [followed by several titles] Abul-Muzaffar Iltutmish [followed by titles].

[With this inscription] the *surat Al-Fath* and *surat Al-Rahman* are [also written],
but have broken down in many places and become indecipherable. In former times the
number of steps within it was 360. Now 335 steps are left. The twenty-five steps of
the top storey are broken. Its height is 90 yards and its perimeter 55 yards.

Behind the Quwwat-ul-Islam mosque is the tomb of Shams-ud-Din Altamash.
On the outside, above the *mihrab* in the northern doorway, the *surat* 'Verily we have
granted a victory' [is written] till the *ayat* 'a destination' [48:1–6]. Below this the *surat*
'The believers must eventually win through' is written till 'they will dwell therein
forever.' [23:1–11] And above the *mihrab* of the eastern doorway, the *surat* 'Glory to
Allah who' till 'mighty arrogance' [is written] [17:1–4]. Below this [the *surat*] 'Verily we
have granted a victory' is written till 'the highest achievement.' [48:1–5] The *surat Al-
Rahman* till the first 'will ye deny' is written below this [55:1–13]. Under this, 'Not equal
are the Companions of the Fire' till 'He is the Exalted in Might, the Wise' [is written]
[59:20–24]. Above the western doorway, the *surat* 'Praise be to Allah, Who created the
heavens and the earth' is written till the *ayat* 'ye deluded away from the Truth' [35:1–3].
Below this [is written:] 'It is part of the Mercy of Allah' till 'then shall every soul receive
its due and none shall be dealt with unjustly.' [3:159–61] Inside the dome, the *surat Al-
Mulk* [is written] till 'little thanks it is ye give.' [67:1–23] Below this, towards the inside,
on the western wall, 'Muhammad is no more than a messenger' [is written] till 'against
those that resist Faith.' [3:144–47] Under this the *surat* 'listen, then, to the inspiration'
[is written] [20:13]. Below this [is written] the *ayat* 'That this is indeed a quran Most
Honourable' till 'from the Lord of the Worlds.' [56:77–80] And below this [is written]: 'He
will forgive you your sins, and admit you to Gardens' till 'that is indeed the Supreme
Achievement.' [61:12] On the right and left of the *mihrab* the 99 names of the Exalted

---

285 Zafar Hasan, Vol. III, p. 7.

Truth [Allah] are written, along with the *ayat* 'Say: O Allah! Lord of Power' up to 'the Lord of majesty and bounty.'[286] Under this [are written]: 'Every soul shall have a taste of death' [21:35], the *ayat Al-Kursi*, the *kalima-e-tayyib* and the *surah* 'His are all things in the heavens and on earth' till 'Nor doth give guidance to a people unjust.' [2:255 –58] And: 'Say: Verily, my Lord hath guided me' till 'He is indeed Oft-forgiving, Most Merciful.' [6:161 –64] And the *ayat* 'Man We did create from a quintessence of clay' till 'We certainly are able to drain it off' [is written] [23:12 –18]

Near the tower is the tomb of Imam Mashhadi, alias Imam Zamin. The following is inscribed on its doorway:

> In the name of Allah, Most Gracious, Most Merciful.
> May continual praise of God and prayer be offered by the residents of the sacred
> enclosure and the dwellers in this favourite tomb as a sacrifice to God, whose
> friends have sacrificed this world and the next in His path and made of the
> immense treasures of life and heart a sacrifice to His court. May manifold praises
> reach the sweetly scented and illumined grave of the intercessor on the Day of
> Judgement [i.e. Muhammad the Prophet], and his pure descendants and friends,
> and his holiness the charitable and announcer of good news to the world, who
> made the divine grace the friend of his holiness, the guide of men and chosen of
> Muhammad, [named] Muhammad 'Ali of the Chishtia sect, descendant of Husain,
> a support to the great Syeds, the best of the revered devotees of God, a Jesus of
> the world of recluse and asceticism, a Moses of the mountain of retirement and
> asceticism, a Moses of the mountain of retirement and seclusion, helped from
> God Who is rich, the pole star of religion and the faith, and a Syed descended
> from Hasan and Husain, in that he erected this holy and elegant building and left
> his parting advice that when his life … should come to an end and favoured with
> the call, 'Enter therein [paradise] in peace and security', it should fly to the sacred
> enclosure and favourite garden, this celebrated building should become the bright
> tomb of his holiness. This building was completed in the year 944 [1537–8].[287]

---

[286] The first quotation is from the Quran (3:26), but, as Qasimi notes in the footnote to the Persian text, the latter phrase cannot be found in that *surah*.

[287] Zafar Hasan, Vol. III, pp. 19–20.

Under the dome on the western wall [is written]:

In the name of Allah
There is no God but Allah, and Muhammad is His Messenger.
Allah is great.

Inside the *mihrab* in the Kufic script is written: 'There is no God but Allah, and Muhammad is His Messenger'. Below this, in a circular pattern, the names of Allah the Most Exalted are written.

To the north from here is the temple of Jogmayaji, which is a place of worship for the Hindus.[288] This temple is located within a *pucca* enclosure. After this, on the road to the *dargah* of Khwaja Qutb-ud-Din, is a gateway. This is called 'Qutb Sahib ki pahli chaukhat' [the first threshold of Qutb Sahib]. Close to it is the tomb of Adham Khan, which is popularly known as Bhool Bhulaiyan. Here in *basi* stone is engraved:

In the name of Allah, Most Gracious, Most Merciful. Zakariya and Yahya
constructed [the grave of] Aqa Jauhar. 1185 *Hijri* [1771–72]

Inscriptions at the tomb of Adham Khan, also known as Bhool Bhulaiyan

On the sides of this tomb are twenty-four doors. On both sides of the doors, above the *mihrabs*, the *kalima-e-tayyib* [is written]. Above another door, the names of Allah the Most Exalted [are written]. Inside the dome, above the *mihrabs* of the eight openings, the *surat Al-Mulk* is written till 'a group' [67:1–8] Inside, on the western wall [is written]:

A.L.R. These are the symbols (or verses) of the perspicuous Book. We have sent
it down as an Arabic Quran, in order that ye may learn wisdom. We do relate unto
thee the most beautiful of stories, in that We reveal to thee this (portion of the)
Quran: before this, thou too was among those who knew it not. [12:1–3]

After this is the *dargah* of Hazrat Khwaja Qutb-ud-Din Bakhtiyar Kaki. The insription on the west-facing first entrance is:

---

[288] The Jogmaya temple is dedicated to Jogmaya, the sister of the God Krishna.

[1] People acquired the treasure of felicity here; at last Shakir Khan threaded the pearls of supplication.

[2] I enquired of myself, 'what shall I write for its date?' Rizwan [the gardener of paradise] said to my heart, 'The secrets of the gate of paradise'. 1119 [1707–08].

On the second, eastern door of the compound, towards Mulla Mauj, in the Sulus script is written.

[1] In the time of the king of the world of Islam, this door to the sky was raised.

[2] Although heaven has a hundred doors, there is no door like it.

[3] A Shaikh who laid the foundations of this door can be titled a second Joseph.

[4] When I asked after the date and name, it said, '*dargah* of the Khwaja of the *qutbs*'. [958/1515]

On the third, northern door, which is close to the Majlis Khana, this chronogram is inscribed:

[1] During the reign of the sun of the sky of empire [named] Sher Shah, the king, having the moon for his standard, the stars for his army, and heaven for his slave,

[2] The majestic tomb, in respect of which the saying 'This is the door of the house of peace' is verified,

[3] Was completed in the year 948 [1541–42], under the superintendence of the Shaikh, the cherisher of religion, Khalilul Haq.[289]

On the marble latticed screen of the entrance to the enclosure of the *dargah*, which lies next to the grave of Maulvi Fakhr-ud-Din, may Allah have mercy on him, is engraved:

Allah   Muhammad   Abu Bakr   'Umar   'Usman   'Ali   Allah

Below this is written:

---

289 Zafar Hasan, Vol. III, pp. 26–27.

[1] On the order of the king of the world, the king of men, Emperor Farrukhsiyar, the nine skies enslaved to him.

[2] The *qutb* of the nine skies turns around the grave of the Khwaja of the faith. Men and angels go around his tomb too.

[3] This beautiful and well-arranged sanctuary was constructed to be like the holiest *qibla* and the most sacred Ka'ba.

On the eastern entrance to this enclosure is engraved:

Allah   Muhammad   Muhammad   Allah

Above the third entrance:

Allah   Muhammad   Abu Bakr   'Usman   'Ali   Allah

Under this is engraved:

[1] Through the effort of the lowliest of the slaves of Shahryar. By the faith and trust in the perfect standard.

[2] The pure ones left for the paradise of Eden. They got the date, the enclosure of the paradise of Eden. [1130/1717–18]

On the right-hand side [is written]: 'Under the supervision of the lowest of slaves in the seventh year of the reign of Farrukh Shah.' On the left-hand side [is written]: 'completed in 1130 *Hijri* [1717–18]. Written by 'Abd-ullah *Shirin Raqm*.'

Inside the *dargah*, on a tiled wall at the head of the grave, the *kalima-e-tayyib* is written. And the date of death of Khwaja Qutb-ud-Din, i.e. Monday, 14 Rabi'-ul-Awwal, 633 *Hijri* [1235] is written on it. Close to the grave of Khwaja Qutb-ud-Din are the graves of Haji Haramain and others. Towards the foot of the grave of Khwaja Qutb-ud-Din, outside the marble enclosure, is the grave of Qazi Hamid-ud-Din Nagauri.[290] The

---

[290] A Sufi saint of the Suhrawardi order, Hamid-ud-Din Nagauri was a close companion of Bakhtiyar Kaki. He died in 1245.

grave's headstone has this written on it: 'Behold! verily on the friends of Allah there is no fear, nor shall they grieve; Those who believe and (constantly) guard against evil.' [10:62–63] On the right-hand side [it says]: 'There will be no death for the people of Allah; no horror of the grave; no terror on the day of judgement.' On the left-hand side [it says]: 'Verily We have granted thee a manifest Victory: That Allah may forgive thee thy faults of the past and those to follow; fulfil His favour to thee; and guide thee on the Straight Way.' [48:1–2]

Towards the top, on the back of the wall with the lamp niche [it says]:

This radiant mausoleum is of the *qutb* of the *auliya* in heaven [followed by several honorifics] Shaikh Hameed-ud-Din Nurullah and it was built by the friend of the poor Suleiman, son of Shaikh Bhika, in the year 694 on the death of the honourable Shaikh [followed by several honorifics] Muhammad Hameed Nurullah during the night of Monday, the eleventh of Ramzan. 'In praise of that comes the sun.' 695 *Hijri*

The inscription on the top of the grave of Maulvi Fakhr-ud-Din, may Allah have mercy on him, [is]:

[1] In the name of Allah, Most Gracious, Most Merciful. There is no God but Allah, and Muhammad is His Messenger.

[2] When Fakhr-ud-Din left the transitory world, that *qutb* of the eternal world offered him a place at his threshold.

[3] When I enquired of the invisible one the year of the death of that moon, the unseen crier said, 'The sun of both worlds.' [1199/1784–84]

Composed by Syed-ush-shu'ara [sic] [poet laureate] Fakhr-ud-Din, the accepted of God. 1222 [1807–08].[291]

At the foot of the grave of Maulana Fakhr-ud-Din is the grave of Jawahar Khan, which has the following inscription:

---

[291] Zafar Hasan, Vol. III, p. 41.

[1] The Khan who was religious and knew by heart the whole Quran, departed from the transitory world.

[2] The invisible crier said, for the date of his death, 'Jawahar Khan was the accepted of God'.[292]

The inscription on the grave of Mahaldar Khan: on the headstone the *ayat Al-Kursi* is written along with 'All that is on earth will perish'. [55:26] The inscription on the *dalan* of Nawab Mumtaz Mahal Begam Sahiba:

[1] Mumtaz Mahal, the *nawab* of heavenly dignity, the source of generosity and munificence, and having good qualities and disposition,

[2] Built with true faith an excellent house of brick at the dargah of Shah Qutb-ud-Din.

[3] Zafar enquired of the mason of wisdom the date of its erection, and he forthwith answered him: 'Say, worthy of paradise'. [1227/1812–13][293]

On the grave of Nawab Zabita Khan the *ayat Al-Kursi* and the *kalima* are written. The mosque of the *dargah* of Hazrat Khwaja Qutb-ud-Din bears the following inscription on the central arch:

[1] His exalted majesty the king Farrukhsiyar, the emperor, who is master of the neck [of the people] and favoured [by God].

[2] Built a beautiful mosque with good intention and firm faith as a worshipping place for old and young.

[3] The invisible crier whispered into the ears of wisdom the chronogram of its erection: 'The accepted abode of God'.[294]

Within the first enclosure of the *dargah* of Qutb Sahib is the tomb of Mu'tamid Khan, the gate of which bears the following inscription:

---

[292] Ibid., p. 42. The chronogram gives the date 1164 *Hijri* (1750–51); Qasimi, p. 256.

[293] Zafar Hasan, Vol. III, pp. 44–45. The *dalan* was built by Mumtaz Mahal, the chief consort of Akbar II.

[294] Ibid., p. 38. The chronogram as worked out by Qasimi gives 1130 *Hijri* (1718–19); Qasimi, p. 256.

[1] During the reign of the manifestation of God, the king 'Alamgir Muhaiuddin [sic], through whose justice body and soul are in the cradle of peace,

[2] Mu'tamad Khan selected [for his burial place] the dust of the feet of Shah Qutb-ud-Din, through the blessing of whose proximity he has hope of the pardon of God.

[3] Everyone in his neighbourhood shines with his light, and the day of judgement will be luminous like the moon by the brightness of his forehead.

[4] Now, O God! Forgive him [Mu'tamad Khan] for he is near to his [Qutb-ud-Din's] feet, and make his soul bright with the light of the pole star of God.

[5] When I enquired of the angels the date of its [the enclosure's] erection, they replied 'O God, make the end good'.[295]

Outside the compound, next to the western gate that has been mentioned earlier, towards the north, is the tomb of Murad Bakhsh. On it is written:

The guiding *pir*, Allah, Muhammad and 'Ali, Fatima, Hasan and Husain, may peace be upon them! The protecting saint Ghaus-ul-A'zam.

[1] Thanks be, that during the reign of Shah 'Alam, the asylum of the worlds, Murad Bakhsh, with truth and sincerity,

[2] Erected a convent [*khanqah*] and a mosque before the *dargah* of the pole star of religion and the world.

[3] When I enquired of wisdom the chronogram, it said: 'She built this mosque and convent'. [1215/1800–01][296]

Inside the tomb, on the arch of the mosque, the same inscription is repeated. In front of this arch, to the south, is the door to the tomb of Hazrat Shah 'Alam Badshah 'Firdaus Manzil'. On it is written:

---

295 Zafar Hasan, Vol. III, p. 29. Mu'tamid Khan was a nobleman at the court of Aurangzeb. The chronogram gives 1048 *Hijri* (1673–74).

296 Ibid., pp. 30–31. Murad Bakhsh was the wife of Shah 'Alam II.

[1] This is the holy tomb of a just king, and this doorway of the *dargah* of the king of religion, the perfect *qutb*.

[2] I asked Syed-ush-shu'ara [*sic*] [the poet laureate] the date of its erection. He at once said, 'This is the door of Firdaus Manzil'.[297]

Within this enclosure of marble are two graves. One is of 'Firdaus Manzil', the other is of Bahadur Shah. At its head is written:

> According to the saying of Mustafa [a name of the Prophet] may Shah 'Alam be rewarded by heaven for his good intentions.
> Ghulam Hayat Khan. The year 1124 [1712–13].[298]

On the headstone of the grave of Badshah 'Ali Gauhar 'Firdaus Manzil' is inscribed:

> He is the forgiver and pardoner
> And may God make paradise his [Shah 'Alam's] residence.
> The year 1221
> He is merciful.

[1] Alas, the sun[299] of the zenith of the royal dignity has been concealed below the earth by the gloom of the eclipse of death.

[2] That is to say, Shah 'Alam, the protector of the world, departed from this world to the pleasure ground of paradise.

[3] O Syed, my miracle-working pen has written a verse, each line of which is a chronogram thereof.

---

[297] Ibid., p. 33. The chronogram gives the date 1221 *Hijri* (1806). The chronogram is a clever play on words, because 'Firdaus Manzil' also means the house of paradise.

[298] Ibid., p. 33.

[299] Shah 'Alam was also a poet, and used the *takhallus* 'Aftab' or sun.

[4] He was a sun on the face of the earth before this. Alas that the sun is buried under the earth.

The scribe Mir Kallan. The year 1221 [1806–07].[300]

Towards the head of the grave, on the headstone is written: 'In the name of Allah, Most Gracious, Most Merciful.' On both sides of the headstone the *ayat Al-Kursi* is written. On the top of the headstone is written:

All that is on earth will perish: But will abide for ever the Face of thy Lord, full of Majesty, Bounty and Honour. [55:26–27]

The houses of Huzur-e-Wala are located here.[301] There is the Diwan-e-Khas and connected buildings. There are other houses, of the *murshidzadas*, from where these people watch the fairs of the *phulwalas*, *chhadis* and the *'urs*. Near the house of Mirza Salim Bahadur is the tomb of Khunkhwar Sahib. On the headstone of his grave the *kalima-e-tayyib* is written.

Near the tomb of Mulla Mauj, in Lado Sarai, the *haveli* of Khwaja Qutb-ud-Din is located in the area of Old Dehli. Connected to this is the tomb of Maulana Jamali. Within it, inscribed all over, is this *ghazal*:

[1] Even if our wickedness may approach to blasphemy, still we cherish hope of your pardon.

[2] At your threshold we are ashamed because your dogs cannot rest at night on account of our wailing.

[3] If I should have the honour to approach the curtain of your secret, an angel will be proud to act as our porter.

[4] Covered with the dust of your street we look contemptible to [common] people, but this meanness is an honour in the estimation of persons of wisdom.

---

300 Zafar Hasan, Vol. III, p. 34.

301 The emperor at the time of writing was Akbar II. His palace near the *dargah* is the complex being referred to. Today this is better known as Zafar Mahal.

[5] By the cloud of your kindness the dust of sin has been washed away, but the blot of our shame could not be cleansed.

[6] On the day of separation from you, in helplessness and loneliness, nothing consoles us but the sorrow we feel for you.

[7] O Jamali! Resort for protection to the door of the friend, for our refuge is the door of the beloved.

The second *ghazal*.

[1] Our restlessness in your love has passed all bounds; our hope is that you will pity our weeping.

[2] How could your pardon be known, had we not shown ourselves to be guilty!

[3] Although we are deserving of wrath for our guiltiness yet we have hope from your kindness.

[4] We may attain the honour, glory and dignity of angels if you observe our humility.

[5] If we become the holder of your secrets, an angel will not be worthy of acting as our porter.

[6] By one shower from the cloud of beneficence you wash away the dust of crime from our ashamed faces.

[7] Cast your eyes upon Jamali with kindness, and do not look at his idleness and shortcomings.

A quatrain:

[1] O thou, whose mercy won the game from wrath, and whose kindness ordered rage to depart!

[2] Wherever there is talk of thy immense forgiveness, people's sin is not weighed there against barely [i.e. it is of little consequence].[302]

---

[302] Zafar Hasan, Vol. III, pp. 91–92. Shaikh Fazlullah, better known as Maulana Jamali, was a Sufi and a poet who was close to Sikandar Lodi as well as the early Mughal rulers. He died in 1535. His tomb is popularly known as Jamali Kamali.

On the western wall the *kalima-e-tayyib* is written, and under it:

> There is no God but He: That is the witness of Allah, His angels, and those endued with knowledge, standing firm on justice. There is no God but He, the Exalted in Power, the Wise. [3:18]

Below this the *kalima-e-tayyib* and, on the headstone of the grave, the *kalima* [again] and the names of Allah the Most Exalted are written.

On the grave next to it, the same *ayat* and *kalima* are written. Apart from this, the date of the death of Maulana Jamali, i.e. 942 *Hijri* [1535–36] is written.

From here towards the *jharna* is the garden of Manzur 'Ali Khan, which is known as Bagh-e-Nazir. On its gate is written:

> In the name of Allah, Most Gracious, Most Merciful.
> [1] In compliance with the order of Muhammad Shah the just, on whose head rests the holy crown.
> [2] A flower garden was planted at the Qutb, the flowers of which are praised by the gardener of paradise.
> [3] May, by the blessings of Suras 'Sad' and 'Tabarak', Roz Afzun be ever prosperous.
> [4] For its date and year the invisible crier said, 'By God, God the Creator is blessed'.
> The year 1161 of the sacred and holy *Hijra*. The twenty-first year of the auspicious reign of Muhammad Shah. [1748–49][303]

The *jharna* is towards the west of this place. It was built by Emperor Muhammad

---

[303] Ibid., p. 98. Roz Afzun was the *Nazir* or chief eunuch during the reign of Muhammad Shah. He evidently built the garden, which at the time of writing was in the possession of Manzur 'Ali Khan.

Shah. The *dalans* here have now been constructed by Huzur-e-Wala Muhammad Akbar Shah.[304] At this spring there is a grave on which is written:

[1] 'Abid who was wise, learned, pious and grave was martyred by a dishonest robber.

[2] The invisible crier told me the chronogram of his death: 'The soul of 'Abid the martyr entered paradise'.[305]

At this location there is also the Kamli Shah ka Takiya, several *khanqahs* and graves. There is the Chahaltan Mazar.[306] On the Shamsi Talab is a mosque called the Auliya Masjid.[307] Near the Shamsi Talab is a domed building. On a red-sandstone piece in this building is the mark of a horseshoe. It is said that this is the mark of the horseshoe of Maula Mushkil Kusha Hazrat 'Ali's horse.[308] 'Only Allah is wise.'

All around this tank [Shamsi Talab] there are the graves of several elders. Hence, to the south are the graves of Qazi 'Abdullah Maqdar Baranji (761 *Hijri*) and Maulana Sama-ud-Din.[309] To the north is the grave of Hazrat Shaikh 'Abdul Haq Muhaddis Dehlavi.[310] Inside the dome of this grave, above the upper *mihrab*, the following inscription is written in the Sulus script:

In the name of Allah, Most Gracious, Most Merciful.

A summary of the happenings of miracles of this exemplary person of our times, the glorious personage, Abul-Majd 'Abdul Haq, may Allah's mercy be upon him. He

---

[304] The first buildings at the *jharna* were actually built by Nawab Ghazi-ud-Din Khan around 1700. Later, Akbar II and Bahadur Shah II added more pavilions.

[305] Zafar Hasan, Vol. III, p. 59. The chronogram gives the date 1209 *Hijri* (1794–95).

[306] The site, known as Chihaltan Chihalman, is believed to be the burial ground of forty Sufis, known as the 'Abdals.

[307] This mosque has great significance as it is believed that the two great Sufi saints, Muin-ud-Din Chishti and Qutb-ud-Din Bakhtiyar Kaki, offered prayers here.

[308] Zafar Hasan says this is believed to be the mark of Prophet Muhammad's horse, who appeared in a dream to Emperor Iltutmish, advising him to build a *hauz* or tank here, in 1229–30. Zafar Hasan, Vol. III, p. 98.

[309] Maulana Sama-ud-Din was a well-known Sufi of the Suhrawardi order; he died in 1495–96.

[310] A well-known Sufi saint and scholar, 'Abdul Haq Muhaddis Dehlavi died in 1642.

was the source of knowledge by the favour of Truth and a determined seeker of knowledge. More plentiful knowledge of the divine sciences he obtained in his twenty-second year by when he also memorized the Quran. He sat on the seat of teaching and was received by divine absorption in the freshness of his youth. After getting his heart away from family and the world he travelled to the two holy mosques. For a long time he studied at these honoured places. He kept the company of the *qutbs* of the time and the great Friends of God. He bid farewell to his specialized training as a teacher of students and apart from that he completed his studies in the Hadith and he returned to his country. For fifty-two years he became well established in the assemblies of the material and the spiritual. He carried out the training of his children and his students. He was engaged in spreading the sciences of the signs and the blessed knowledge of Hadith. No one among the moderns or the ancients among the *'Ulama* of Iran did assist him. He became distinguished and exceptional. Particularly of the knowledge of Hadith he wrote several books. As a result the *Ulama* of the time studied him closely [...] His profuse writings go into hundreds of volumes and thousands of verses. In the Muharram of 958 this shadow of appearance fell on the base world and in the year 1052 *Hijri* this broad forehead went away to the the world of purity. The date of his birth is 'Shaikh of the Auliya' and the date of his death 'Pride of the world'.

Under this, in a circular pattern, the *ayat Al-Kursi* is written seven times. Below it on a wall towards the back the *kalima-e-tayyib* is written.

This is the *mauza-e-Mehrauli* which is the property of the *khadims* of the *dargah* Qutb Sahib and the Jats, and others. To the north of this is *mauza-e-Malikpur*. Here is the tomb of Sultan Garhi. Above the entrance of this tomb is written:

He secured this patch of blessed ground, the exalted sultan, the greatest king of kings [followed by several titles] (the lettering is ruined here) in the two worlds, the sultan of sultans [followed by several titles] by the providence of the Lord of the two worlds, Abul Muzaffar Altamash Sultan Naasir-ud-Din [followed by titles] in the year 627.

On the threshold of this entrance the *ayat Al-Kursi* is written till 'to dwell therein forever.' [2:255–57] And below it [is written]: 'There is no God but Allah, the Sovereign, the evident Truth. Muhammad is the messenger of Allah, the Truth Speaker among the Firsts.' Below this [is written]: 'The mosques of Allah shall be visited' till 'Allah guides not those who do wrong.' [9:18–19] The following *ayat* [is written] above the *mihrab* on the mosque's western wall: 'Verily We have granted thee a victory' till 'the highest achievement.' [48:1–5] Below this [is written] the complete *ayat* 'The first House of worship appointed for men' [3:96]. On both sides of the *mihrab* the names of Allah are written in a special script.

Here there are four graves in a pit. One is the grave of Nasir-ud-Din Ghazi;[311] the second that of his brother; the third that of his sister; and the fourth is that of the emperor's concubine. The '*urs* of this Sultan is on 18 Shawwal.

[At this point the main narrative comes to an end. The following seems to be a series of postscripts. The arrangement is entirely haphazard, and the dates of some of the inscriptions show that they must have been put into the original book years later.]

The details of Jantar Mantar are as follows

Mirza Akhtarullah and three Hindu gentlemen of Jaipur were involved in its construction. They built it according to instructions. The said Mirza was accomplished in the knowledge of mathematics and lived during the reign of Muhammad Shah. He was a servant of Jai Singh. In that era, Mubshar Khan used to derive questions according to the astronomical tables of Ulugh Begi and give his opinion. All sages used to agree with these and there used to be no mistakes. As it happened, the time-period of these astronomical tables, which was 300 years, expired and errors started coming into the predictions of Mubshar Khan. Whatever he predicted would turn out incorrect. After giving it much thought he said to the emperor, 'These astronomical tables have become defective and their time limit, which was 300 years, has come to an end. Therefore the predictions are incorrect.' For this reason he requested the emperor to command Mirza Khairullah to prepare other astronomical tables. Following the advice of the said Khan the emperor sent a message to Jai Singh in this regard: that Mirza Khairullah should be made to prepare a set of astronomical tables as this is the wish of the emperor. The

---

[311] The son of Emperor Iltutmish, Nasir-ud-Din, died within his father's lifetime.

emperor also penned some words of favour and kindness for Raja Sawai. In short, at the command of the emperor, Raja Sawai related this entire affair to the said Mirza and showed great consideration towards him. He had the astronomical tables prepared and despatched them to Emperor Muhammad Shah. The emperor handed these tables to Mubshar Khan. The said Khan started deriving predictions from these tables and these predictions proved correct. There was not even a hair's breadth of error in them. Whatever the writer has heard, he has written.

Near Lal Bangla is the grave of Gir Bai, who was the paramour of Syed 'Abdullah Khan. The following couplet is engraved on her grave:

[1] The adulterous woman went under the earth. It was appropriate that grass was less than the pure world.

The following verses are written on the dwelling of Miyan Sabir Bakhsh:

[1] O King, forgive our crime. We are criminal and you a forgiver.

[2] You do good, and we are wrongdoers. We commit immoderate and unpunishable crimes.

[3] Not a single blameless moment has passed unto me. In the presence of such a heart, I do not pray.

[4] At the door comes the runaway slave. Among the sinners he dishonours himself.

[5] That you will forgive me, is the hope I have at your pleasure. From that hope I say to myself, 'Do not despair.'

[6] The sea of your favours is endless. Those who have lost hope in your mercy are the devil.

[7] The lower self and the devil strike in my path. May your favours be. I am the seeker of your intercession.

The mosque of Shaikh Bayazidullahu is located in Sabzi Mandi. Inside, on a plate, the following is engraved: 'The most excellent *zikr*: there is no God but Allah, and Muhammad is His Messenger.'

The *kalima-e-tayyib* is written above the *mihrab* in Kambalposhaan's mosque in the Sulus script.

It is said that that this inscription was written on the grave of the poet Mirza Bedil. The grave was located outside the Dehli Gate but now no trace of it remains.

[1] Before this Sa'di Shirazi had said: 'Bedil is unique – what more can one say?'

The following *qit'a* [couplet-sequence] is engraved on a marble tablet in the Naskh script, inside the *bangla* opposite the Qadam Sharif:

[1] From the mortal world, like the wave of the deep sea, Durdana Khanam has left for the abode of peace.

[2] The year of her death, I asked, O heart, from the mystery and the prophetic voice replied: 'Without doubt her abode is in heaven.' [1223/1808–09]

The following inscription is engraved in the Nast'aliq script on *basi* stone above the entrance of that enclosure which faces the first door of the Qadam Sharif:

[1] May Allah have mercy on him who has left this world. The prophetic voice said, 'it became paradise one day.' [1234/1818–19]

The following is written in the Nast'aliq script above the western entrance of the *madarsa* of Nawab Ghazi-ud-Din Khan:

There remains no mark on the tablet but the reward of an act and a good name. In the blessed memory of Nawab I'tmad-ud-Daulah Zia-ul-Mulk Syed Fazl-e-'Ali Khan Bahadur Sohrab Jang, who entrusted the Honourable English East India Company with one lakh and seventy thousand rupees for the advancement of learning at this school, situated in Delhi proper, his native place, [this tablet] was inscribed in 1829. Written by Syed Amir Rizwi.[312]

On a mosque located on the road to Sayyid Hasan Rasul Numa the following chronogram is written in Persian:

[1] In the reign of the second Sahib Qiran Muhammad Shah, the sun and moon kissed his stirrups.

[2] Like the eyebrows of the beloved in the country of Dehli, he constructed a well-made mosque as a pious deed.

[3] The nib of the pearl-stringing pen wrote its year and date: 'The edifice appeared of a moonlit, life-giving mosque.' [1156/1743–44]

Behind Pahar Ganj, towards the west there is a mosque. Above its three entrances these inscriptions are written. Above the northern door towards the side is written:

Granted by the Truth, said a voice from heaven from the purity of its heart, granted by the Truth.

There is a mosque whose foundation was laid from the first day on piety. [9:108]

Granted by the Truth. It is the Aqsa mosque and the Holy Ka'ba. 1039 [1629]

Below this, inside the *mihrab* [is written]: 'O Allah. O Muhammad. O All Powerful One.'

To the north of this entrance, on the right, towards the side is written:

[1] The four friends of Muhammad who are the holy crown. Like the four letters of 'Muhammad' they are friends of each other.

On the left, towards the side [is written]:

[1] Get up my heart from the introxication: Abu Bakr and 'Umar, 'Usman and Haidar.

Above the third entrance, on the south-eastern side, in this manner is written:

Granted by the Truth. Granted by the Truth. For the poor, the door to Allah. Granted by the Truth. Granted by the Truth.

Inside the mosque, above the *mihrab* of the large middle entrance, is written:

O Guide.

[1] Everyone at this doorstep is received with purpose. The crown of felicity is placed on his head.

---

[312] Zafar Hasan, Vol. II, p. 1.

O Guide.

At the place where the *pesh imam* stands, inside the *mihrab*, in the Sulus script is written:

> In the name of Allah, Most Gracious, Most Merciful. Whoever says 'there is no God but Allah, and Muhammad is His Messenger' will enter paradise.

On both sides the inscription 'Guide' is written.

There was an old mosque outside the Khidki Γarash Khana, no trace of which remains. It had a chronogram written on it:

> [1] May the purest ones descend on this mosque. And may the pen shower pearls on its every letter.
>
> [2] When I asked the prophetic voice about its date, it said; 'like Shah Hatim's name may it also be eternal.' [920/1514–15]

The well of Qasim Khan is located inside the city. On a marble slab in it is the chronogram written in Nasta'liq script:

> [1] Qasim Khan bought with his life the well of gold and with his heart made a bequest of it.
>
> [2] The prophetic voice spoke its date thus: 'the life-giving water is bequeathed to all.' [1191/1777]

On the city's outskirts, near the old Idgah, this is written on a garden wall:

> It is hoped that whoever is buried in this holy place is forgiven. It was constructed on the fifteenth of blessed Muharram in the year 834 [1430].

On the road to Pahar Ganj, towards the east, near the Ajmeri Gate and the *madarsa* of Nawab Ghazi-ud-Din Khan, is a mosque. Above its door is engraved:

> [1] About the year of the mosque of wisdom, the prophetic voice said: 'Like the Ka'ba, full of blessings.' [1110/1698]

A couplet is written thus:

> [1] Anyone that comes to the head of this desolate grave of ours must illumine this house of mine with the Fatiha.

After this, on a marble tablet, the following is inscribed in the Nasta'liq script:

[1] From the birth of that pearl of pure descent, in one thousand and fifty-one *Hijri* of the Prophet's time.

[2] On the twentieth of the month of fasting, from the womb of the shell, the pearl was born.

[3] When the lance of death it received from fate, it was like the moon hiding in a cloud of dust.

[4] When I asked the prophetic voice, it cried that 'Muhammad 'Ali resides now in paradise.' [1095/1683]

The grave of Muhammad Amin Khan outside Ajmeri Gate bears a chronogram:

[1] The dark clay of this existence has no permanence. How then does one trust the turn of time?

[2] In trust of the faith of Muhammad, the flag of its rule: like the sun it flew high from the east to the west.

[3] On the *saqi*'s orders he swallowed the drink which makes both the high and the low lose their senses.

[4] When his pure soul left for the eternal paradise, there like the beloveds it was given the status of the head of the assembly of nobles.

[5] The mind spoke of the date of this event thus: 'He was the *wazir* Shah Nishan and a defender of Islam.' [1133/1719–20]

[6] O God, in honour of the Messenger, Abu Bakr and 'Umar, 'Usman and Haidar,

[7] By the woman of the last day [Fatima] and her two sons, grant safety on the Day of Judgment.

[8] Following the world's way, I'timad-ud-Daulah, after embellishing the work of faith left for paradise.

[9] When his soul united with the divine mercy, the date of his death too became 'united with mercy.' [1138/1725]

The inscription on the grave of Sayyid Hasan Rasul Numa, which is written in the Sulus script on a marble tablet:

Hasan Rasul Numa, the most glorious of the descendants of Husain, the second Owais Qarani and the third Hasnain. [1103/1691–92]

Over the arch of the east-facing doorway inside the tomb [is written]:

Rasul Numa remained firm with the Prophet. [1103/1691–92] Written by the sinning slave Yaqut Raqam Khan alias 'Ibadullah.[313]

Inscriptions at tombs located outside the city

On a *basi*-stone tablet in the Nasta'liq script: 'In the name of Allah, Most Gracious, Most Merciful. He is the Ever-Living One Who never dies'.

This grave is located outside Burhan-ul-Mulk's enclosure:

> This is the grave of Aqa Beg Mashhadi, son of the Mirza Mas'ud whom God took into His mercy. The date of death of the departed one is the month of Jamadi-us-Sani, 1193 *Hijri*.
>
> [1] With a hundred desires, he left this mortal world and in youth itself he carried his heart from the world.

On the outskirts of the city, on a marble tablet in the Sulus script, the following *ayat* is engraved: 'All that is on earth will perish: But will abide (for ever) the Face of thy Lord, full of Majesty, Bounty and Honour'. [55:26–27]

This grave is located outside Burhan-ul-Mulk's enclosure:

> [1] Alas, Qasim Beg was martyred in plain youth. The pain of his passing will always live in the hearts of the old and the young.
>
> [2] Since he lost his life fighting the unbelievers, by excellent right the garden of paradise was necessary for him.
>
> [3] Being a martyr, he joins the servitude of Husain. *Houris* and *ghilman* are worthy of being servants at his court.
>
> [4] At the time of his death, the prophetic voice said not to grieve. The grace of Hazrat Qasim will always be on him.
>
> [5] Because from Karbala Haidar bestowed on him the crown and said, 'may Qasim Beg's resurrection be with Qasim the sultan of the faith'. [1171/1757–58]

The verses are inscribed in the Persian script.

> The death of the one now in God's mercy and accepted of God, Qasim Beg and Aqa

---

313 Zafar Hasan, Vol. II, p. 231.

Wali, son of 'Abbas Beg, was written on Monday, the twenty-second of Shawwal of the Prophetic *Hijri* calendar.

This is written in the Sulus script.

On the Neeli Chhatri outside the city, below Salimgarh, is this inscription in Nasta'liq on marble inside the *chhatri*, facing the east:

O Protector!

When that emperor, the protector of the world, returned from the delightful country of Kashmir and honoured this place of grace with his presence, he ordered that this verse should also be engraved:

Humayun Shah, son of Shah Babar, whose pure blood is from Sahib Qiran [Taimur]. The sixteenth year of the propitious reign of Jahangir, corresponding to 1030 [1620–21]

O Revealer!

At the time when the king of the seven climes, Nur-ud-Din Jahangir, the king champion of faith, started from his capital Agra for paradise-like Kashmir, this verse came to his inspired tongue. The impromptu verse of Jahangir Shah the great: What a graceful and happy place, the seat of Jannat Ashyani.

The fourteenth year of the reign of Jahangir corresponding to 1028 [1618–19].[314]

Located in the sands is a grave at Shaikh Muhammad's platform. Its inscription is:

In the name of Allah, Most Gracious, Most Merciful. My God may my contentiousness be forgotten through the *talqin* ['dictation' to the dead] so that the grave is a resting place and one rests in it. May Allah's blessings be upon the Prophet, his heirs, the chaste one [Fatima], the two grandsons [in Persian:] there is no death [?] Salah Khan in Ramzan [?] and Al-Sajjad, Al-Baqir, Al-Sadiq, Al-Kazim, Al-Riza, Al-Naqi, Al-Nafi and Al-'Askari [Shi'i *imams*], may Allah's blessings be upon them all.

[1] In the time of the Great Caliph, Allah eternalized His Beneficial Essence.

[2] This holy place the like of which is not there, was constructed by:

[3] The Shaikh of Islam, traveller to the two sanctuaries; the Shaikh of the people of the Traditions by consensus.

---

[314] Zafar Hasan, Vol. II, p. 299.

[4] Shaikh 'Abd-ul-Nabi Nu'mani, the lodestar of knowledge and the source of gains.

[5] The year and date of this beneficent building, the mind asks, and it replied: 'an excellent place.' [983/1575]

There is a mosque near the *haveli* of Nawab Mahabat Khan on which the following chronogram is engraved in the Sulus script: above the three *mihrabs* of the mosque: 'There is no God but Allah, and Muhammad is His Messenger.' On one side of the *mihrab* (in the middle) are written 'O Opener' and 'Glory be to Allah.' On the courtyard wall in both directions in the Kufic script, 'The Sovereign' is written. Inside the *mihrab*, at the place where the *imam* stands [is written]: 'There is no God but Allah, and Muhammad is His Messenger.' Above the entrance of the mosque, 'O Opener' is written.

The inscription in the old mosque is the same one as the Katra Maidagaran's and is engraved in *basi* stone in Nasta'liq. The house of Miyan Sabir Bakhsh is also located here. Towards the right, in the Sulus script, is written: 'Commemorate Allah as ye have been directed' [1133/1720–21]. Inside the *mihrab*, above the entrance, in *tughra* style [is written]: 'There is no God but Allah, and Muhammad is His Messenger.' Towards the left, in *tughra* style, are written:

Allah   Muhammad   Abu Bakr   'Umar
'Usman and Fatima   Hasan and Husain

On the grave at Miya Sabir Bakhsh's house two tablets are fixed. On one of them, in the Sulus script [is written]:

The well-known slave among sinners, in the year 1100 since the *hijrat* [flight] of the Prophet, may Allah's blessings be upon him.

On the second tablet, above the eastern entrance to the kitchen of the auspicious *khanqah*, in the Nasta'liq script is written: 'The accepted gift from the Messenger, may Allah's blessings be upon him.' The source of these two stone tablets could not be ascertained.

On the mosque at Miyan Sabir Bakhsh's house [is written]: 'Turn then Thy face in the direction of the sacred Mosque' [2:144]. Inside Miyan Sabir Bakhsh's mosque, in the Sulus script, is inscribed: 'In the name of Allah, Most Gracious, Most Merciful. A house and destination of abundance.' [1134/1721–22] Inside the mosque, the *kalima-e-tayyib* and the word 'Allah' are written in the Arabic script.

In the Ganj Mir Khan there is a house. Above its entrance on a marble tablet, in the Naskh script, is engraved:

> [1] By the favour and generosity, the door of Jamshed's palace is readied. Till the
>   Last Day it will remain firm and upright.

Near the house of Nawab Qalandar 'Ali Bakhsh is a garden. Above its entrance, in *tughra* style, is written: 'May Allah appoint a place for him in paradise.' [1270 /1853–54] [Here] there are two tablets in *basi* stone. One of these was installed by Miyan Sabir Bakhsh in his mosque. The second tablet is located near the Dehli Gate. Both tablets have inscriptions in the Sulus and Persian scripts:

> Allah   Muhammad
>
> In the name of Allah, Most Gracious, Most Merciful.
>
> Say: 'O my Servants who have transgressed against their souls! Despair not of the
> Mercy of Allah: for Allah forgives all sins: for He is Oft-Forgiving, Most Merciful.'
>
> [39:53]

Along with this, five couplets from the *Pandnama* are inscribed.

Two graves are located here. One is made of marble, the other of *basi* stone. On the first grave are inscribed the complete 'In the name of Allah', 'All that is on earth will perish' [55:26], the *kalima* and the *ayat Al-Kursi*. The *kalima-e-tayyib* is written on the second grave. Near the blessed ruins there is a grave. Here on a red-stone tablet, in the Sulus script, is inscribed: 'Allah announced paradise for his servamts.'

In and around the *dargah* of Khwaja Baqi Billah are many graves with the following inscriptions. In Naskh and Nasta'liq [scripts] are engraved:

> In the name of Allah, Most Gracious, Most Merciful. There is no God but Allah, and
> Muhammad is His Messenger. Muhammad Sardar Khan. On the seventh of Rajab
> 1188 Hijri [14 September 1774] he united with the Truth.

This inscription is engraved inside the *dargah* of Khwaja Baqi Billah on a marble tablet in the Nasta'liq script:

> In the name of Allah, Most Gracious, Most Merciful. There is no God but Allah, and
> Muhammad is His Messenger. On the twenty-third of the month of Sha'ban, 'Alam
> Beg Khan the martyr from the mortal world united with the eternal world.
> 1193 [1779]

The following inscription is engraved on the grave of Khwaja Baqi Billah in Nasta'liq [script]:

>In the name of Allah, Most Gracious, Most Merciful.
>
>[1] Alas! That noble Sayyid from whose munificence the whole world profited, on the judgement of the sky, has left the world.
>
>[2] When I asked intelligence the date of his passing away, it said: 'Zain-ud-Din Muhammad Khan joined the people of paradise.' [1166/1752–53]

This inscription is engraved in marble on one of the graves inside the Khwaja Baqi Billah *dargah*:

>Allah is great. There is no God but Allah, and Muhammad is His Messenger.
>
>[1] Khwaja Muhammad happily set off for the Garden in the month of Ramzan.
>
>[2] Then the dreamer in the heart of his admirers sent this revelation: he was *maqbul* before, now he is *mahmud*. [1161/1747–48]

On one side of the shrine of Khwaja Baqi Billah, the following is inscribed in marble in Nasta'liq [script]:

>Ahmad Baqi on the twenty-third day of Shawwal, 1143 *Hijri*, was united with the mercy of Truth. [30 April 1731]

The following inscriptions are located outside the *dargah* of Khwaja Baqi Billah. This inscription is on *basi* stone in Nasta'liq [script]:

>Khwaja Nurullah Khan Naqshbandi, son of Imam Ja'far Sadiq, and grandson of Sayyid Ahmad Kashani, twenty-first of Zil-Hajj, 1236 *Hijri* [18 September 1821].

The following is written in a clear script on a *basi*-stone tablet:

>He is the Forgiver. The death of Shah Pasand Khan, son of Shah Nawaz Khan, of Afghan descent, happened on the second of Rabi'-ul-Awwal, 1245 *Hijri* [31 August 1829]

This inscription is written outside the Khwaja Baqi Billah [complex] on a red-stone tablet in *tughra* style: 'They died before dying', followed by the *kalima-e-tayyib*. This inscription is outside the Khwaja Baqi Billah [complex] on *basi* stone:

>In the name of Allah, Most Gracious, Most Merciful. The date of death of Khwaja Ghulam Baha-ud-Din, son of Khwaja Zain-ud-Din is 1164 *Hijri* [1750–51].
>
>[1] Since he always sought God's eternal pleasure, therefore his date [of death] is 'seeker of the eternal paradise.' [1164/1750–51]

The grave of Ghulam Muhammad Khan is located in Katra Badi. On a red-stone tablet on it, in Sulus [script], is written:

> [1] What a blessed grave it is of the Khan-e-Khanan Amjad, who is the commander of the army of the faith and is of the family of the Sultan of Mashhad.
>
> [2] His name was Ghulam Ahmad and the year of his departure becomes 'the slave of Muhammad'. [1163/1749–50]

On a grave outside the enclosure of Burhan-ul-Mulk is an inscription in *basi* stone in the Sulus script:

> All that is on earth will perish: But will abide for ever the Face of thy Lord. [55:26–27]
>
> [1] Alas, the injustice of the oppression of the [heavenly] sphere, that in youth this young man became desireless.
>
> [2] The oppressive sky gave him the wound of the musket, and destroyed the house of this lowest world.
>
> [3] Since, upon his life, he was Shi'a, of the 'people of the cloak', the Sayyid of the martyrs places a crown on his head.
>
> [4] The prophetic voice spake the date of his death: 'may he be resurrected with the martyrs of Karbala'. [1136/1723–24]

The following is inscribed in Persian:

> The date of passing on of Mirza Mughal Beg into God's mercy is the second of Shawwal, 1196 *Hijri*. [9 September 1782]

It is in the Sulus script.

This grave is located within the tomb of Burhan-ul-Mulk:

> Allah   Muhammad   'Ali   Fatima   Husain   Hasan
>
> [1] O woe that Mirza Hasan is martyred at the hands of the irreligious. May he be forgiven like Husain and the Karbala martyrs.
>
> [2] He appeared in the battlefield and was struck by the vile unbelievers. His life was shut in the fort of the mercy of Truth.
>
> [3] Intoxicated always with the wine of the *saqi* of Kausar, may he be intoxicated with the wine of the sun of the family of Mustafa.
>
> [4] He was martyred and for the sake of forgiveness, by the sun of the king of the faith, on the Last Day, may there be a *manshur* in his hands for his martyrdom.

[5] As for his dates, the heart, filling with sadness, said: 'with Husain, with Hasan, may Mirza Hasan be resurrected.' [1185/1772–73]

These verses are inscribed in Persian and on the grave the *ayat Al-Kursi* is also engraved.

This grave is located within Burhan-ul-Mulk's tomb. Here, on a *basi*-stone tablet, in the Sulus script, is written:

All that is on earth will perish: But will abide for ever the Face of thy Lord, full of Majesty, Bounty and Honour. [55:26–27]

[1] Alas when Aqa Wali Khan departed from this world towards the other:

[2] The family of the Messenger [i.e. Prophet Muhammad] were mourners, and the whole world cried a hundred dirges for him.

[3] Intelligence wrote down the date of his death: 'may he be resurrected with the God's favourite.' [1190/1776–77]

These verses are engraved in Persian.

[Also:]

The death of the departed Aqa Wali Beg Khan, son of 'Abbas Beg, is on the night of Thursday, twenty-seventh of Jamadi-us-Sani.

On the outskirts of the city, inside the *dargah* of Khwaja Sahib [Baqi Billah] which is located next to the old Idgah, an inscription of a grave in the enclosure [reads]:
[The inscription is not recorded by the scribe.]

This grave is located within the *dargah* of Khwaja Baqi Billah. On the side of the grave, which is next to the grave of Hazrat Janaza Parran, is inscribed in red stone:

This is the grave of Jalal-ud-Din, may God hallow his secret.

The first line:

This is a holy enclosure and auspicious grave. It was by the famous 'Imad Salar Badayuni, with Mirza Katib-e-Wahi, who, due to the accidents of life from his country [the lettering is broken from here].

The second line is broken.

The third line:

The grave of Jalal was made in this blessed enclosure. It is hoped that whoever is buried in this enclosure will be forgiven. The date of the construction of this place is twenty-fifth of the holy Muharram, 834 [12 October 1430].

Above the eastern entrance [is written]:

In the name of Allah, Most Gracious, Most Merciful. Whoever enters it attains security; Pilgrimage thereto is a duty men owe to Allah, those who can afford the journey; but if any deny faith, Allah stands not in need of any of His creatures. [3:97]

Above the northern entrance, in *basi* stone, is inscribed:

In the name of Allah, Most Gracious, Most Merciful. But Allah doth call to the Home of Peace: He doth guide whom He pleaseth to a way that is straight. [10:25]

In the year 592 [indecipherable] by the high order of the revered Sultan, the strength of the world and the faith, Muhammad bin Saam Nasir, commander of the faithful.

On a marble tablet, in the Nasta'liq script [is written]:

There is no God but Allah, and Muhammad is His Messenger, may blessings and peace be upon him.

[1] When Mehr-un-Nisa, the Begam of good character, who, like the sun, illumines the eternal world;

[2] She left the world and left the world in darkness. She cast a shadow on the realm of eternity.

[3] I asked the date of her death from the obliged. By a hundred efforts, and pain, sorrow and suffering,

[4] He lamented without end, and said: 'Alas, alas, Mehr-un-Nisa.' [1229/1814]

On the house of Zinat *tawaif* near the *baoli* in Shah Mardan, on marble in the Nasta'liq script is written:

[1] When this new building was made, it gained the adornment of the feet of Hazrat Shah.

[2] Its date was said to be: 'This place was constructed with the pleasure of God.' [1216/1801–02]

There is a grave outside the gate of Shah Mardan. Here, on a *basi*-stone plate, in the Sulus script, is inscribed:

[1] I asked intelligence for the date of his death: 'may the sinless one be resurrected with the third Imam.' [950/1543–44]

The Naqqar Khana of Shah Mardan bears the following inscription:

[1] When Sadiq 'Ali built a high edifice at the threshold of Haidar [a title of 'Ali]

[2] For the date of the foundation of the edifice, Sadiq said, 'The drum House of Haidar.' [1230/1814–15][315]

There is a tomb near Jantar Mantar. On its south-facing gate is an inscription in the Nasta'liq script on a marble tablet:

The one who comes to this place shall receive forgiveness. May he remember 'Abdullah Mir Muhammad 'Ali, son of Mir Muhammad Sakht Kaman Al-Husaini with the Fatiha. The date of death of the above-mentioned Mir is the tenth of Ramzan 1095 *Hijri* [20 August 1684].

Muhammad 'Ali departed for 'Ali's abode in 1095 *Hijri*.

Inside the garden, facing the south, is written in Nasta'liq [script]:

Say: O my Servants who have transgressed … (till) … He is Oft-Forgiving, Most Merciful. [39:53]

Praise be to Allah, the Cherisher and Sustainer of the worlds … (till) … who go not astray. [1:2–7]

In the name of Allah, Most Gracious, Most Merciful. (And the complete *surah*:)

Say: He is Allah, the One and Only… [112].

Inside the garden, facing the east, in Nasta'liq is written:

There is no God but Allah, and Muhammad is His Messenger. O Allah send blessings upon Muhammad and his family as many as are all the particles and a thousand times of 'Call out to 'Ali, He is able to bring about the extraordinary. You will find him an effective supporter in all calamities. All worries and sorrows will soon disappear on account of your authority, O 'Ali, O 'Ali, O 'Ali.'

Inside the garden, facing the east, in Nasta'liq [is written]:

Just as that blessed hair of the Sayyid of the two forms of existence, may Allah's blessings and peace be upon him, and of the Shah-e-Mardan Murtaza 'Ali, by the means of Mah Bano Begam from the family of Sayyid Shah 'Ali Al-Herati along with this most contemptible one, Rahmiya Bano, daughter of the late Sayyid Mirza, was received. In the hope of intercession they were kept at this place so that anyone

---

[315] Zafar Hasan, Vol. II, p. 196. Qasimi gives a slightly different date: 1229 *Hijri* (1813–14).

who is exalted by this honour prays well for this powerless woman and if anyone carries away this holy relic, on the day of reckoning he would be [deemed] the Prophet's criminal and be shamed before him.

At Qutb Sahib, the following inscription is written on the eastern wall of Zabita Khan's *dalan*. It is affixed on the grave of Hameed-ud-Din Khan. It is engraved in *musa* stone on marble in Naskh [script]:

As to those who believe and work righteous deeds, they have, for their entertainment, the Gardens of Paradise. [18:107]

The date of passing away of Hameed-ud-Din Khan Bahadur of the reign of 'Alamgir, son of the late Sardar Khan, son of Baqi Khan, is the eighth of Safar, 1141 *Hijri*, Monday, in the second half of the day [12 September 1728]. The day is derived from 'he departed from the mortal world to the eternal'. His honourable age was sixty-three years and five months.

And above the entrance of the *khanqah* it is written in *musa* stone on marble, in the Nasta'liq script:

I have prepared this tomb for myself. May it never be that this place be sold, passed on or granted away and within the enclosure of this indigent one may no other grave be built. I have appointed my son Muhammad 'Abdullah as its *mutawalli* [trustee]. And composed for it: 'Hameed-ud-Din Khan Bahadur of the reign of 'Alamgir. 1137 *Hijri* [1724–25].

At Shah Mardan, on a red-stone tablet 'In the name of Allah' and the *kalima-e-tayyib* are written, along with these verses in the Nasta'liq script:

[1]   Alas that after us in this world several flowers will bloom and springs will come.

[2]   People who never knew us will come and pass by our grave.

On the twenty-first of Zil-Hajj, Miyan 'Ishrat Sahib, may he be forgiven, united with the mercy of the Truth. 1078 [1667–68]

At Shah Mardan, this inscription is engraved on a *basi*-stone tablet in the Nasta'liq script:

Nawab Ibrahim Beg Khan Bahadur, son of Ihtisham-ud-Daulah Nawab Isma'il Beg Khan Bahadur Firoz Jang died on the fifth of Jamadi-us-Sani 1244 *Hijri* [12 December 1828].

On the grave of the wife of Bakhshi Mahmud Khan, located near the grave of Nawab Najaf Khan, this inscription is written on a marble tablet in the Nasta'liq script:

[1] Alas, she left this impermanent world, that angelic, good-natured woman.

[2] In devotion, the namesake of the daughter of the Messenger: may she be forgiven in the name of the soul of Fatima the Splendid One.

[3] In her heart she was devoted in the highest degree to the *wilayat* of 'Ali. She was lost in the devotion to the name of the most honourable Imams.

[4] She was the daughter of Najaf Khan, the Mir Bakhshi of India. May God grant her the purest of abodes.

[5] I drew in a woeful sigh and the verse of her date manifested: 'may 'Ali and Fatima be her intercessors on the day of reckoning.' [1234/1820–21]

The inscription on the marble headstone of the grave facing the *dargah* of Shah Mardan, which is engraved in Nasta'liq script, [is]:

[1] Mahaldar Begam, who used to say that prostrating before the 'people of the house' was her religion,

[2] The sorrow for her has dried up the hearts of her friends. And in mourning for her the eyes of the believers have become wet.

[3] This Sayyid woman herself told this Sayyid about her date of departure: 'I am the palace-dweller of the eternal paradise.' [1219/1804–05]

In front of the *dargah* Shah Mastan, the following verse is written on the grave of Hisam-ud-Din Haidar's mother: 'In heaven may she be among the leaders and be the leader of the women.' This inscription is engraved on a marble headstone in Nasta'liq [script]:

He is the Exalted One.

[1] My name is Sadat Khan, known as Kazim, when 'Kazim's slave' departed from this world:

[2] The Sayyid spoke in his language the verse of his year: 'The defender of this wrongdoer is Imam Kazim.' [1219/1804–05]

This inscription is engraved in Nasta'liq [script] on a marble headstone on one side:

[1] The Nawab of the heaven-granted high status, Sayyid and leader of the pious.

[2] When he died, ah! the date of his death emerged: 'may his abode be at the feet of 'Ali.' [1190/1776–77]

In the Sulus script on marble [is written]:

> In the name of Allah, Most Gracious, Most Merciful. Allah. Muhammad. 'Ali.
> Fatima. Hasan. Husain. 'Ali. Muhammad. Ja'far. Musa. 'Ali. Muhammad. 'Ali. Hasan.
> Muhammad. May peace be upon them.
>
> The date of death of Sharf-un-Nisa Begam, alias Haji Begam, daughter of Mirza
> Sayyid Muhammad Gulistana alias Mirza Khani is the twelfth of Rabi'-us-Sani,
> Sunday, 1216 [21 August 1801].

In the Shah Mardan [complex] in the Sulus script [is written]:

> In the name of Allah, Most Gracious, Most Merciful. O Forgiver of sinners. O Veiler
> of faults.

On both sides [of this] is engraved:

> [1] When Mirza Muhsin departed this mortal place, he went to sleep under the
> holy footprint of the Shah-e-Mardan.
>
> [2] He was called by the Truth and the Sayyid spoke his date of death thus: 'may
> Muhsin be resurrected with Husain and Hasan.' [1197/1782–83]
>
> In a dream he spoke of his own grave: Mirza Muhsin Quli Khan, 1197 *Hijri*.

In Sultanji [near Nizam-ud-Din Auliya's *dargah*], facing the Majlis Khana, is Munshi Amir-ud-Din's grave, which has an inscription on a *basi*-stone tablet in the Nasta'liq script:

> [1] Amir-ud-Din Muhammad was a cause for pride among us, when he departed
> the world of sorrow for paradise.
>
> [2] Then, I sought the *Hijri* year of his passing: it turned out to be two hundred and
> fifty more than a thousand. [1250/1834–35]

This is written on the grave of the daughter of the heir-apparent in Lal Bangla, on a *basi*-stone tablet, in the Sulus script: 'O Forgiver' and the complete 'In the name of Allah . . .' The *kalima-e-tayyib* is written in *tughra* style and the following verses are written in the Sulus script:

> [1] Alas, Zeenat Al-Zamani Begam, has left this world for the eternal realm.
>
> [2] My heart bled at that and burned with that brand. 'The branding of the crying
> heart', I thus spoke its date. [1247/1831–32]

'O Ever-Living One' and 'O Self-Existing One' are written on the marble headstone in the Sulus script.

The grave of the wife of the heir-apparent is also at Lal Bangla. On a marble tablet on this grave the *kalima-e-tayyib* is written in *tughra* style, followed by these verses in the Sulus script:

[1] He opened a beginning in eternity, when you travelled. You strive for salvation from Allah and hope for serenity.

[2] Bu Zafar was invoked to give the correct date: 'You are the only forgiveness who loves forgiveness.'

On the marble headstone of the grave, in *tughra* style, is written:

All that is on earth will perish: But will abide for ever the Face of thy Lord, full of Majesty, Bounty and Honour. [55:26–27]

In the Sulus script the *kalima-e-tayyib* is written, and on all four sides a few *ayats* of the *surat Al-Mulk* are written in the same script.

On another grave located in Lal Bangla, on a marble tablet, the whole 'In the name of Allah...' is written, along with the following in *tughra* style:

I bear witness that there is none worthy of worship except Allah, the One alone, without partner and I bear witness that Muhammad is His servant and messenger.

And in the Naskh script the following verses are engraved:

[1] Alas, Ashraf-un-Nisa Khanam has died. May God grant her a place in the Garden of Eden.

[2] When the heart pulled in a chest-scratching sigh, her date of death too came to be 'chest-scratching sigh.' [1226/1811–12]

Inside the *burj* at Lal Bangla, on the coating of lime on all sides, the *surat* 'Blessed be He' [*surat Al-Mulk*] is written in the Sulus script. Outside the *burj* on all sides the *kalima-e-tayyib* is written on the blue dome.

Near the grave of Muhammad Shah's wife, on another grave, is written in Nasta'liq [script]:

[1] This tomb resembles paradise and is with a symmetrical window. Like the heavenly palace is a pleasing place.

[2] When this place manifested before the people's eyes, the connoisseurs come to look at its sights.

[3] When it has this status of a pleasing place, I spoke to the intelligent about the date of its construction: 'what a place, what a lovely place.' [948/1541–41]

The inscription at Husain Chishti:

He is Allah, the Prosperous One.

For us Allah sufficeth, and He is the best disposer of affairs. [3:173]

[1] All praise is for Allah who is indeed the Truth. He favoured us with the Prophet.

[2] Of the year of the laying of its foundation, intelligence said, 'Ali's appearance' has come to be. [1221/1806–07]

On the road to Shah Mardan is the grave of Hafiz Hafeez. On the lime-coated headstone is written in Nasta'liq [script]:

[1] Love spake the date of his death with great sadness: 'Muhammad Hafeez was the eulogist of the family of the Prophet.' [1249/1833–34]

On one side of the grave is written [in Urdu]:

[1] Whoever goes this way to Shah Mardan, O God, may he read the Fatiha at this grave. (Written by [missing].)

This *qit'a* [couplet-sequence] is written on the Mussamman Burj:

[1] O thou who hast fetters on thy legs and a padlock on thy heart, beware! And O thou who hast thine eyelids sewn up and feet in the mire, beware!

[2] Bound towards the west and having thy face to the east, O traveller who hast turned thy back on thy destination, beware![316]

On Shah Jahan's *khwabgah* it is written:

Allah is pure! How beautiful are these painted mansions and charming residences. They are a part of the high heaven. I may say the high-souled holy angels are desirous of looking at them; if the residents of different parts and directions of the world should come to walk around them, as [they walk] round the old house [Ka'ba] it would be allowable; or if the beholders of the two worlds should run to kiss their highly

---

[316] Zafar Hasan, Vol. I, p. 18. This octagonal building, projecting from the west wall of the Red Fort, was where the emperor used to give *jharokha darshan*, i.e. show himself to his subjects.

glorious threshold as [they kiss] the black stone (of the Ka'ba), it would be proper. The commencement of this great fort, which is higher than the palace of the heavens and is the envy of the wall of Alexander; and of this pleasant edifice, and of the Hayat Bakhsh [life-bestowing] garden, which is to these buildings as the soul is to the body, and the lamp to an assembly; and of the pure canal, the limpid water of which is to the person possessing sight as a mirror showing the world, and to the wise, the unveiler of the secret world; and of the water cascades, each of which you may say is the whiteness of the dawn, or a tablet containing secrets of the Tablet and Pen [of Fate]; and of the fountains, each of which is a hand of light inclined to shake hands with the inhabitants of the heavens, or is a string of bright pearls made to descend to reward the inhabitants of the earth; and of the tank, full to the brim of the water of life and in its purity the envy of light and the spring of the sun, announced on 12 of Zil-Hajj in the twelfth year of the holy ascension, corresponding to 1048 *Hijri* [16 April 1639], the tidings of happiness to men. The completion of it, at the expense of fifty lakhs of rupees, by the power of the auspicious feet of the sovereign of the earth, the lord of the world, the originator of these heavenly buildings, Shihab-ud-

Din Muhammad, the lord of felicity, Shah Jahan, the king, the champion of the faith, opened on the 24 Rabi'-ul-Awwal in the twenty-first blessed year of the ascension, corresponding to 1058 *Hijri* [18 April 1648], the door of grace to the world.[317]

[1]   The emperor of the heavens, the king of the world, Shah Jahan. Under the auspices of the second Sahib Qiran [Shah Jahan].

[2]   In the royal palace there are hundreds of maginificences. Like the sun in the sky may they always shine.

[3]   Its foundations are such that its construction is firm: just like the blessed palace of God's throne.

[4]   How heart-alluringly is the palace adorned. A right garden of paradise adorned with a hundred qualities.

[5]   Nobility is an *ayat* in praise of its grandeur. Felicity is in the embrace of its galleries.

[6]   Prostrations in this *sarai* of exhilaration are made by the drinker's forehead far from any wine.

[7]   Its stairs are anointed with rectitude by every one, like the river Jun whose honour flows and increases.

[8]   When its walls are paved, it shows a mirror to the sun's face.

[9]   When the face of the walls is adorned, it causes envy to Chinese engravers.

[10] When for its sake the hand of time works, heaven its heights tries to ensnare.

[11] From its fountains and water tanks, by the ground water everything is cleansed till the sky.

[12] As was the place of the Just Emperor, such are the palaces of this Emperor.

On the mosque near the Khidki Farash Khana:

[1]   This mosque which is the Ka'ba of religious persons: may its foundation be extant as long as Islam exists.

[2]   Whoever submissively runs to its threshold, if he has no fear of sin, it may be permissible.

[3]   Khair-un-Nisa who is the founder of the *qibla* of prayer has ever the face of her heart towards God.

---

317 Ibid., pp. 16–17. The *khwabgah* lies just within the Musamman Burj.

[4] That Syed lady who is good and artless is one of the selected descendants of Yahya Hashimi.

[5] When I asked wisdom the date of its foundation, it replied, 'say it is the mosque of Khair-un-Nisa'.[318] [1071/1660–61]

The inscription in Nasta'liq [script] on the Sunehri Masjid opposite the Dehli Gate:

[1] Thanks be to God! In the reign of Ahmad Shah, who is a champion of the faith, a king, a cherisher of the people, a doer of justice, and a protection to the kings of the world.

[2] *Nawab-e-Qudsi* [of divine] dignity built this mosque; may the common favour of that place of adoration of angels be everlasting.

[3] The exertions of the courteous and benevolent Nawab Bahadur Javed, of exalted power, constructed such an edifice.

[4] The clean well and tank of its court are an honour to Zamzam, whoever washed himself with its water became clean of his sins.

[5] How beautifully Khurram obtained the year of its foundation! From the invisible inspiration, 'The mosque of Jerusalem, the rising place of divine light'.[319]

The chronogram on the Masjid Mahratan at the Hauz Qazi is written in the Nasta'liq script:

[1] Come here, O travellers of the mystic path that this place is for the servants of the place of prostration.

[2] Ye asked for the date and knowing its value: 'from this door emerges the hidden path to the Ka'ba'. [1268/1851–52]

The inscription of the mosque of Masita Zardoz which is in the Chhatta Jan Nisar [is]:

[1] He built this place of worship for God and accomplished a good task for the last day.

[2] Sohrab gave its date in this way: 'He built this Masita mosque and the well'. [sic]

---

318 Ibid., p. 89.

319 Ibid., p. 29. The chronogram gives the date 1164 *Hijri* (1750–51).

The chronogram of the Masjid Muhammad Khan, located at Lal Kuan, is:

[1] When this *sarai* of worship was built by the favour of the Lord of Greatness,

[2] The prophetic voice spoke the verse of its date of construction: 'Muhammad Khan got this mosque constructed.' [1203/1788–89]

On the mosque of the Peepal ka Kuan is this chronogram in the Nasta'liq script:

[1] In the reign of Akbar Shah, the mosque was constructed by a man called Isma'il of the Shahsun clan.

[2] He also built his own grave in its courtyard. May the illustrious God be pleased with him.

[3] The date of constructing this place of worship: 'The pure end, no more, no less.' [1224/1809–10]

The inscription of this mosque is in Nasta'liq which Fazl 'Ali Khan constructed anew:

[1] As Nawab I'timad-ud-Daulah, his abode is high, Sayyid Fazl 'Ali Khan constructed this mosque.

[2] Wanting to know the date of its construction, a voice came from a corner of the heart: '*Qibla* for the people with vision, a Ka'ba for the pure ones.' [*sic*]

Illustrations